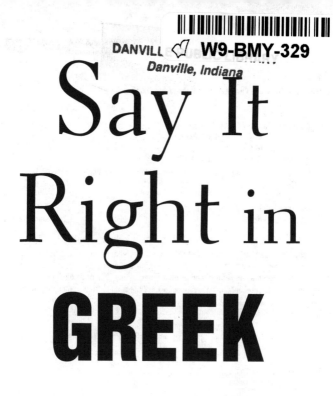

DANVILLE PUBLIC LIBRARY
Danville, Indiana

Say It Right in GREEK

Easily Pronounced Language Systems

Clyde Peters

McGraw Hill

New York   Chicago   San Francisco   Lisbon   London   Madrid   Mexico City
Milan   New Delhi   San Juan   Seoul   Singapore   Sydney   Toronto

The McGraw·Hill Companies

Library of Congress Cataloging-in-Publication Data

Chapman, Betty.
   Say it right in Greek / Betty Chapman and Clyde Peters.
         p.   cm. — (Say it right)
     Includes index.
     ISBN 0-07-170141-9 (alk. paper)
      1. Greek language, Modern—Pronunciation.   I. Peters, Clyde (Clyde Elias)
  II. Title.

   PA1063.C48   2009
   489'.3152—dc22   2009046352

Copyright © 2010 by EPLS Publishing. All rights reserved. Printed in the United States of America. Except as permitted under the United States Copyright Act of 1976, no part of this publication may be reproduced or distributed in any form or by any means, or stored in a database or retrieval system, without the prior written permission of the publisher.

1 2 3 4 5 6 7 8 9 10 11 12 13 14 15   WFR/WFR   1 9 8 7 6 5 4 3 2 1 0

ISBN 978-0-07-170141-9
MHID   0-07-170141-9

McGraw-Hill books are available at special quantity discounts to use as premiums and sales promotions or for use in corporate training programs. To contact a representative, please e-mail us at bulksales@mcgraw-hill.com.

Also available: *Say It Right in Arabic* • *Say It Right in Brazilian Portuguese* • *Say It Right in Chinese* • *Say It Right in Chinese, Audio Edition* • *Say It Right in Dutch* • *Say It Right in French* • *Say It Right in French, Audio Edition* • *Say It Right in German* • *Say It Right in Italian* • *Say It Right in Italian, Audio Edition* • *Say It Right in Japanese* • *Say It Right in Korean* • *Say It Right in Russian* • *Say It Right in Spanish* • *Say It Right in Spanish, Audio Edition* • *Say It Right in Thai* • *Dígalo correctamente en inglés [Say It Right in English]*

Author: Clyde Peters
Illustrations: Luc Nisset
President, EPLS: Betty Chapman, www.isayitright.com
Senior Series Editor: Priscilla Leal Bailey
Greek Language Consultant: Barbara Hawkins

CONTENTS

DANVILLE PUBLIC LIBRARY
Danville, Indiana

INTRODUCTION

The SAY IT RIGHT FOREIGN
LANGUAGE PHRASE BOOK
SERIES has been developed
with the conviction that learning to
speak a foreign language should be fun and easy!

All SAY IT RIGHT phrase books feature the EPLS
Vowel Symbol System, a revolutionary phonetic
system that stresses consistency, clarity, and
above all, simplicity!

Since this unique phonetic system is used in all
SAY IT RIGHT phrase books, you only have to
learn the VOWEL SYMBOL SYSTEM ONCE!

The SAY IT RIGHT series uses the easiest phrases
possible for English speakers to pronounce, and
is designed to reflect how foreign languages are
used by native speakers.

You will be amazed at how confidence in your
pronunciation leads to an eagerness to talk to
other people in their own language.

Whether you want to learn a new language for
travel, education, business, study, or personal
enrichment, SAY IT RIGHT phrase books offer a
simple and effective method of pronunciation and
communication.

PRONUNCIATION GUIDE

Most English speakers are familiar with the Greek word **Zeus.** This is how the correct pronunciation is represented in the EPLS Vowel Symbol System.

All Greek vowel sounds are assigned a specific non-changing symbol. When these symbols are used in conjunction with consonants and read normally, pronunciation of even the most difficult foreign word becomes incredibly EASY!

On the following page are all the EPLS Vowel Symbols used in this book. They are EASY to LEARN since their sounds are familiar. Beneath each symbol are three English words which contain the sound of the symbol.

Practice pronouncing the words under each symbol until you mentally associate the correct vowel sound with the correct symbol. Most symbols are pronounced the way they look!

THE SAME BASIC SYMBOLS ARE USED IN ALL SAY IT RIGHT PHRASE BOOKS!

EPLS VOWEL SYMBOL SYSTEM

(ah)	(ĕ)	(EE)	(O)	(oo)
Calm	Men	See	Oak	Cool
Saw	Red	Feet	Cold	Pool
Law	Bed	Meet	Sold	Too

EPLS CONSONANTS

Most consonants like **T**, **D**, and **S** are straightforward and pronounced like English letters. However, Greek has sounds that have no English equivalents. The following EPLS pronunciation guide letters represent some unique Greek sounds.

Ŗ Pronounce these letter like a Spanish **r**.

G̲ This EPLS letter represents a **gh** sound like in the word **gh**ost. (Page 9)

T̲H̲ Pronounce these letters like the **th** in **th**en.

TH These letters represent the voiced letters in the word **th**in or **th**ink.

Ḧ This **EPLS** letter represents an aspirated sound like in the word **h**elp or **h**ue. (Page 9)

KS These letters are joined together to make and sound like the **ks** in the word kic**ks**.

PS This letter combination sounds like the **ps** in the word chi**ps**.

Greek Alphabet	Letter Name	EPLS Pronunciation
Α α	Άλφα	ahL-Fuh
Β β	Βήτα	VEE-Tah
Γ γ	Γάμμα	Gah-Mah
Δ δ	Δέλτα	THeL-Tah
Ε ε	Έψιλον	e-PSEE-LON
Ζ ζ	Ζήτα	ZEE-Tah
Η η	Ήτα	EE-Tah
Θ ϑ	Θήτα	THEE-Tah
Ι ι	Γιότα	GYO-Tah
Κ κ	Κάππα	Kah-Pah
Λ λ	Λάμδα	LahM-THah
Μ μ	Μι	MEE
Ν ν	Νι	NEE
Ξ ξ	Ξι	KSEE
Ο ο	Όμηκρον	O-MEE-KRON
Π π	Πι	PEE
Ρ ρ	Ρο	RO
Σ σς	Σίγμα	SEEG-Mah
Τ τ	Ταυ	Tah
Υ υ	Ύψιλον	EE-PSEE-LON
Φ φ	Φι	FEE
Χ χ	Χι	HEE
Ψ ψ	Ψι	PSEE
Ω ω	Ωμέγα	O-ME-Gah

Greek Alphabet	Greek Vowels	EPLS	Description
A α	A α	ⓐⱨ	As in **a**ll
B β		V	As in **v**ictor
Γ γ		<u>G</u>	As in **gh**ost
Δ δ		<u>TH</u>	As in **th**en
E ε	E ε	ⓔ̆	As in **e**gg
Z ζ		Z	As in **z**oo
H η	H η	ⓔⒺ	As in f**ee**t
Θ ϑ		TH	As in **th**in
I ι	I ι	ⓔⒺ	As in s**ee**
K κ		K	As in soc**k**
Λ λ		L	As in **l**ive
M μ		M	As in **m**eet
N ν		N	As in **n**ew
Ξ ξ		KS	As in kic**ks**
O o	O o	ⓞ	As in **o**ak
Π π		P	As in **p**ass
P ρ		Ɍ	As in Spanish **r**
Σ σς		S	As in **s**ent
T τ		T	As in was**t**e
Υ υ	Υ υ	ⓔⒺ	As in **e**at
Φ φ		F	As in **f**eel
X χ		Ħ	As in **h**ope
Ψ ψ		PS	As in chi**ps**
Ω ω	Ω ω	ⓞ	As in **o**at

GREEK TO ME!

There are 24 letters in the Greek Alphabet. There are seven double letters that together make one sound and are called diphthongs. You don't have to worry too much about this because EPLS has already interpreted the sound of those two letters in the Vowel Symbol System.

Although at first glance at the Alphabet, your first thought is **"This is Greek to me!"**, there are some letters that you will recognize because they look like letters in the English alphabet and are pronounced the same.

The caveat is that there are a few letters that look like English letters but are pronounced entirely different. Such is the case with the Greek letter P which is pronounced like a rolled Spanish **r**.

The Greek letters γ and χ have no English equivalents. In some cases γ will be pronounced Y as in **y**es and in other cases it will be pronounced G as in English. However, EPLS has enhanced this letter with an underline <u>G</u>. This helps you to remember that the <u>G</u> sound is drawn out when spoken, almost as if there is an **"h"** following it like in the word **gh**ost.

The χ is represented by the EPLS Ḧ which reminds you to aspirate this sound. Practice saying **h**elp, **h**ose, **h**ot.

PRONUNCIATION TIPS

- Each pronunciation guide word is broken into syllables. Read each word slowly, one syllable at a time, increasing speed as you become more familiar with the system.

- In Greek it is important to emphasize certain syllables. This mark (´) **over** the syllable reminds you to **STRESS** that syllable.

- The pronunciation choices in this book were chosen for their simplicity and effectiveness.

- To perfect your Greek accent you must listen closely to Greek speakers and adjust your speech accordingly. Don't forget to practice!

- All of the phrases in this book are written in the Modern Greek alphabet.

- A Greek question mark is indicated by this familiar punctuation mark (;). It looks like and English semicolon. A period is indicated like this (.), the same as in English.

- In Greek language all letters in a word are spoken.

ICONS USED IN THIS BOOK

KEY WORDS

You will find this icon at the beginning of chapters indicating key words relating to chapter content. These are important words to become familiar with.

PHRASEMAKER

The Phrasemaker icon provides the traveler with a choice of phrases that allows the user to make his or her own sentences.

Say It
Right in
GREEK

ESSENTIAL WORDS AND PHRASES

Here are some basic words and phrases that will help you express your needs and feelings in **Greek**.

Hi / Hello

Γειά σας

Y@h-S@hS

How are you?

Τι κάνετε;

T@E K@h-N@-T@

Fine, thank you.

Καλά, ευχαριστώ.

K@h-L@h @F-H@h-R@ES-T@

And you?

Εσείς;

@-S@ES

Good-bye

Γειά σας

Y@h-S@hS

Good morning

Καλημέρα

K⟨ah⟩-L⟨EE⟩-M⟨é⟩-R⟨ah⟩

Good evening

Καλησπέρα

K⟨ah⟩-L⟨EE⟩-SP⟨é⟩-R⟨ah⟩

Good night

Καληνύχτα

K⟨ah⟩-L⟨EE⟩-N⟨EE⟩H-T⟨ah⟩

Mr.

Κύριος

K⟨EE⟩-R⟨EE⟩-⟨O⟩S

Mrs.

Κυρία

K⟨EE⟩-R⟨EE⟩-⟨ah⟩

Miss

Δεσποινίς

TH⟨é⟩S-P⟨EE⟩-N⟨EE⟩S

Generally speaking, the informal is used only among friends so most phrases in this book will be shown in the formal form.

Yes

Ναι

N**ě**

No

Όχι

O-HEE

Please

Παρακαλώ

P**ah**-R**ah**-K**ah**-LO

Thank you

Ευχαριστώ

ěF-H**ah**-REE-STO

You're welcome

Παρακαλώ

P**ah**-R**ah**-K**ah**-LO

Excuse me, please

Με συγχωρείτε, Παρακαλώ

SEE-GNO-MEE　　P**ah**-R**ah**-K**ah**-LO

I'm sorry

Συγνώμη

SEE-GNO-MEE

I don't understand!

Δεν καταλαβαίνω!

TH(ĕ)N K(ah)-T(ah)-L(ah)-V(ĕ)-N(o)

Do you understand?

Καταλαβαίνετε;

K(ah)-T(ah)-L(ah)-V(ĕ)-N(ĕ)-T(ĕ)

I'm a tourist. (m)

Είμαι τουρίστας.

(EE)-M(ĕ) T(oo)-R(EE)S-T(ah)S

I'm a tourist. (f)

Είμαι τουρίστρια.

(EE)-M(ĕ) T(oo)-R(EE)S-TR(EE)-(ah)

I don't understand Greek.

Δεν καταλαβαίνω ελληνικά.

TH(ĕ)N K(ah)-T(ah)-L(ĕ)-V(ĕ)-N(o)
(ĕ)-L(EE)-N(EE)-K(ah)

Do you speak English?

Μιλάτε αγγλικά;

M(EE)-L(ah)-T(ĕ) (ah)N-GL(EE)-K(ah)

Please repeat.

Το ξαναλέτε παρακαλώ.

T(o) KS(ah)N-(ah)-L(ĕ)-T(ĕ) P(ah)-R(ah)-K(ah)-L(o)

FEELINGS

I would like...

Θα ήθελα ...

TH**ah** **EE**-TH**ĕ**-L**ah**...

I have...

Έχω ...

ĕ-H**O**...

I know.

Ξέρω.

KS**ĕ**-R**O**

I don't know.

Δεν ξέρω.

TH**ĕ**N KS**ĕ**-R**O**

I like it.

Μου αρέσει.

M**O** **ah**-R**ĕ**-S**EE**

I don't like it.

Δεν μου αρέσει.

TH**ĕ**N M**O** **ah**-R**ĕ**-S**EE**

I'm lost.

Έχω χαθεί.

Ĕ́-HO H̆ah-THEE

We are lost.

Έχουμε χαθεί.

Ĕ́-Hoo-Mĕ H̆ah-THEE

I'm in a hurry.

Βιάζομαι.

VEE-ah́-ZO-Mĕ

I'm ill. (m)

Είμαι άρρωστος.

EÉ-Mĕ ah́-RO-STOS

I'm ill. (f)

Είμαι άρρωστη.

EÉ-Mĕ ah́-RO-STEE

I'm hungry.

Πεινάω.

PEE-Nah́-O

I'm thirsty.

Δειψάω.

TH̲EEP-Sah́-O

INTRODUCTIONS

Use the following phrases
when meeting someone
for the first time both
privately and in business.

My name is...

Με λένε ...

ΜῈ-LῈ-NῈ...

What's your name?

Πώς σας λένε;

PⓄS SⒶS LῈ-NῈ

Very nice to meet you.

Χαίρω πολύ.

HῈ-ℝⓄ PⓄ-LḖ

Greece is named Hellas Ελλάς, Ελλάςδα in
Greek. It is officially the Hellenic Republic. In 2004
it had the honor of hosting the 2004 Olympics.

WHO IS IT?

I

Εγώ

ⓔ-G̲Ⓞ́

You (Pl) (Plural for many)
(Formal for one)

Εσείς

ⓔ-SⒺⒺ́S

You (Informal)
(Used with good friends)

Εσύ

ⓔ-SⒺⒺ́

He

Αυτός

ⓐⓗF-TⓄ́S

She

Αυτή

ⓐⓗF-TⒺⒺ́

It

Αυτό

ⓐⓗF-TⓄ́

We

Εμείς

ⓔ-MⒺⒺ́S

They

Αυτοί (m) / Αυτές (f) / Αυτά (n)

ⓐⓗF-TⒺⒺ́ / ⓐⓗF-Tⓔ́S / ⓐⓗF-Tⓐⓗ́

THE BIG QUESTIONS

Who?

Ποιος; (m) / Ποια; (f)

P⒠-Ⓞ́S / P⒠-ⓐ́ⓗ

Who is it?

Ποιός είναι; (m) / Ποια είναι; (f)

P⒠-Ⓞ́S ⒠́-Nⓔ̆ / P⒠-ⓐ́ⓗ ⒠́-Nⓔ̆

What?

Τι;

TⒺⒺ

What's this?

Τι είναι αυτό;

TⒺⒺ ⒠́-Nⓔ̆ ⓐ́ⓗF-TⓄ́

When?

Πότε;

PⓄ́-Tⓔ̆

Where?

Που;

Pⓞⓞ

Where is...?

Που είναι;

PO EE-NE

Which?

Ποιό;

PEE-O

Why?

Γιατί;

Yah-TEE

How?

Πώς;

POS

How much? (money)

Πόσο κάνει;

PO-SO Kah-NEE

How long? (time)

Πόσο χρόνο θα πάρει;

PO-SO HRO-NO THah-Pah-EE

ASKING FOR THINGS

The following phrases are valuable for directions, food and help, etc.

I would like...

Θα ήθελα ...

TH⒜ ⒠-TH⒠-L⒜...

I need...

Χρειάζομαι ...

H̃R⒠-⒜-ZO-M⒠...

Can you...?

Μπορείτε ... ;

BO-R⒠-T⒠...

When asking for things be sure to say <u>please</u> and <u>thank you</u>.

Please	**Thank you**
Παρακαλώ	Ευχαριστώ
P⒜-R⒜-K⒜-LO	⒠F-H̃⒜-R⒠-STO

PHRASEMAKER

Combine **I would like...** with the following phrases beneath, and you will have a good idea how to ask for things.

I would like...

Θα ήθελα ...

TH@h €€´-TH@-L@h...

▶ **more coffee**

περισσότερο καφέ

P@-R@€-S@´-T@-R@ K@h-F@´

▶ **some water**

λίγο νερό

L€€´-G@ N@-R@´

▶ **some ice**

λίγο πάγο

L€€´-G@ P@h´-G@

▶ **the menu**

το μενού

T@ M@-N@@´

PHRASEMAKER

Here are a few sentences
you can use when you feel
the urge to say **I need**... or **can you**...?

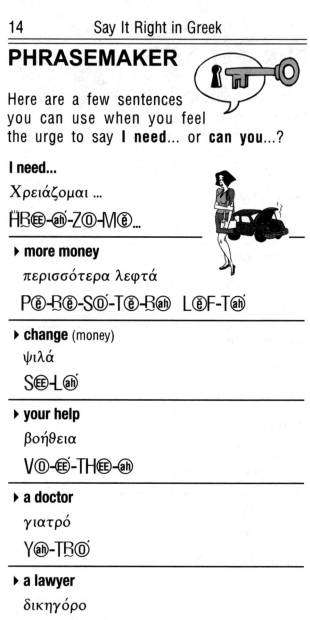

I need...

Χρειάζομαι ...

HREE-ah-ZO-MEe...

▸ **more money**

περισσότερα λεφτά

PEe-REe-SO-TEe-Rah   LEeF-Tah

▸ **change** (money)

ψιλά

SEE-Lah

▸ **your help**

βοήθεια

VO-EE-THEE-ah

▸ **a doctor**

γιατρό

Yah-TRO

▸ **a lawyer**

δικηγόρο

THEE-KEE-GO-RO

PHRASEMAKER

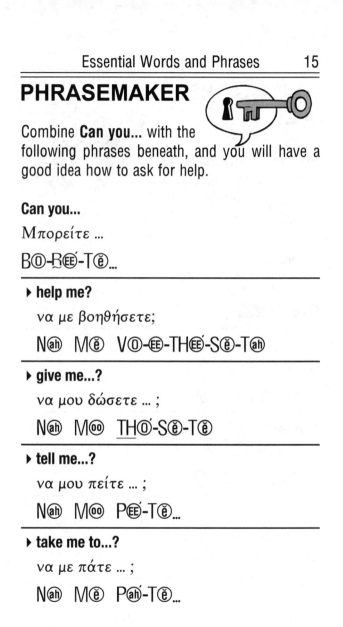

Combine **Can you...** with the
following phrases beneath, and you will have a
good idea how to ask for help.

Can you...

Μπορείτε ...

ΒΟ-ΡΕΈ-ΤΕ...

▸ **help me?**

να με βοηθήσετε;

ΝΑ ΜΕ ΒΟ-ΕΕ-ΤΗΕΈ-ΣΕ-ΤΑΗ

▸ **give me...?**

να μου δώσετε ... ;

ΝΑ ΜΟΟ ΤΗΌ-ΣΕ-ΤΕ

▸ **tell me...?**

να μου πείτε ... ;

ΝΑ ΜΟΟ ΠΕΈ-ΤΕ...

▸ **take me to...?**

να με πάτε ... ;

ΝΑ ΜΕ ΠΑΉ-ΤΕ...

ASKING THE WAY

No matter how independent you are, sooner or later you'll probably have to ask for directions.

Where is...?

Που είναι ... ;

P⓪⓪ ⒠⒠́-N⒠...

I'm looking for...

Ψάχνω για ...

PS⒜⒣ H̃N⓪ Y⒜⒣...

Is it near?

Είναι κοντά;

⒠⒠́-N⒠ K⓪N-D⒜⒣

Is it far?

Είναι μακριά;

⒠⒠́-N⒠ M⒜⒣-KR⒠⒠-⒜⒣

Left	**Right**
Αριστερά	Δεξιά
⒜⒣-R⒠⒠-ST⒠̃-D⒜⒣	TH⒠̃K-S⒠⒠-⒜⒣

PHRASEMAKER

Where is...

Που είναι ...

P⑩ ⒠-N⒠...

▶ **the restroom?**

η τουαλέτα;

⒠ T⑩-⒜-L⒠-T⒜

▶ **the telephone?**

το τηλέφωνο;

T⑩ T⒠-L⒠-F⑩-N⑩

▶ **the beach?**

η παραλία;

⒠ P⒜-R⒜-L⒠-⒜

▶ **the hotel?**

το ξενοδοχείο;

T⑩ KS⒠N-⑩-TH⑩-H⒠-⑩

▶ **the train to...?**

το τρένο για ... ;

T⑩ TR⒠-N⑩ Y⒜...

TIME

What time is it?

Τι ώρα είναι;

TEE O´-Rah EE´-Ne

Morning

Πρωί

PRO-EE´

Noon

Μεσημέρι

ME-SEE-ME´-REE

Night

Νύχτα

NEE´H-Tah

Today

Σήμερα

SEE´-ME-Rah

Tomorrow

Αύριο

ah´V-REE-O

This week

Αυτή την εβδομάδα

ⓐhF-TⓔⒺ́ TⓔⒺN ⓔ̆V-THⓄ-Mⓐh́-THⓐh

This month

Αυτό το μήνα

ⓐhF-TⓄ́N TⓄ MⓔⒺ́-Nⓐh

This year

Εφέτος

ⓔ̆Fⓔ̆́-TⓄS

Now

Τώρα

TⓄ́-Ⓡⓐh

Soon

Σύντομα

SⓔⒺ́N-DⓄ-Mⓐh

Later

Αργότερα

ⓐhⓇ-GⓄ́-Tⓔ̆-Ⓡⓐh

Never

ποτέ

PⓄ-Tⓔ̆́

MASCULINE, FEMININE, AND NEUTER

If a word is masculine, feminine, or neuter it will be indicated by an (m) for masculine and (f) for feminie and (n) for neuter as shown below.

(m) Masculine	(m,s) Masculine singular
	(m,pl) Masculine plural
(f) Feminine	(f,s) Feminine singular
	(f,pl) Feminine plural
(n) Neuter	

Below is an example of the article o / Ⓞ for masculine, η / Ⓔ for feminine, and το / TⓄ for neuter. The article preceding the noun indicates the gender.

Masculine	**the coffee**
	ο καφές
	Ⓞ KⓐⱧ-FⓔˊS
Feminine	**the restroom**
	η τουαλέτα
	Ⓔ TⓄⓄ-ⓐⱧ-Lⓔˊ-TⓐⱧ
Neuter	**the train**
	το τρένο
	TⓄ TRⓔˊ-NⓄ

THE, A (AN), AND SOME

To use the correct form of **The**, **A**, **(An)**, **Some**, or **These** you must know if the Greek word is masculine or feminine. Often you will have to guess! If you make a mistake, you will still be understood.

The

Ο (m,s) / οι (m,pl) / Η (f,s) / οι (f,pl)

Ⓞ / ⒠ / ⒠ / ⒠

Το (n,s) / Τα (n,pl)

TⓄ / Tⓐⓗ

A or **An** (Singular only)

Ο (m,s) / Η (f,s) / Το (n)

Ⓞ / ⒠ / TⓄ

Some

Μερικοί (m) / Μερικες (f) / Μερικά (n)

Mⓔ-Rⓔⓔ-Kⓔⓔ / Mⓔ-Rⓔⓔ-Kⓔ'S / Mⓔ-Rⓔⓔ-Kⓐⓗ

These

Αυτόι (m) / Αυτές (f) / Αυτά (n)

ⓐⓗF-Tⓔⓔ / ⓐⓗF-Tⓔ'S / ⓐⓗF-Tⓐⓗ

USEFUL OPPOSITES

Near	**Far**
Κοντά	Μακριά
KON-Dah	Mah-KREE-ah

Here	**There**
Εδώ	Εκεί
ĕ-THO	ĕ-KEE

Left	**Right**
Αριστερά	Δεξιά
ah-REE-STĕ-Rah	THĕK-SEE-ah

A little	**A lot**
Λίγο	Πολύ
LEE-GO	PO-LEE

More	**Less**
Περισσότερο	Λιγότερο
Pĕ-REE-SO-Tĕ-RO	LEE-GO-Tĕ-RO

Big	**Small**
Μεγάλο	Μικρό
Mĕ-Gah-LO	MEE-KRO

Open	Closed
Ανοικτό	Κλειστό
ah-NEEK-TO	KLEES-TO

Cheap	Expensive
Φτηνό	Ακριβό
FTEE-NO	ah-KREE-VO

Dirty	Clean
Βρώμικο	Καθαρό
VRO-MEE-KO	Kah-THah-RO

Good	Bad
Καλό	Κακό
Kah-LO	Kah-KO

Vacant	Occupied
Ελεύθερο	Πιασμένο
e-LeF-THe-RO	PEE-ah-S-Me-NO

Right	Wrong
Σωστό	Λάθος
SOS-TO	Lah-THOS

WORDS OF ENDEARMENT

I like you.

Μου αρέσεις.

M⑩ ⓐⓗ-Ⓡⓔ́-SⒺⒺS

I love you.

Σε αγαπάω.

Sⓔ́ ⓐⓗ-Gⓐⓗ-Pⓐⓗ-Ⓞ́

I love Greece.

Την αγαπάω την ελλάδα.

TⒺⒺN ⓐⓗ-Gⓐⓗ-Pⓐⓗ-Ⓞ́ TⒺⒺN ⓐⓗ-Lⓐⓗ́-Vⓐⓗ

Male friend

Φίλος

FⒺⒺ́-LⓄS

Female friend

Φίλη

FⒺⒺ́-LⒺⒺ

Kiss me!

Φιλησέ με!

FⒺⒺ-LⒺⒺ-Sⓔ́ Mⓔ́

WORDS OF ANGER

What do you want?

Τι θέλεις;

TΕΕ THĕ́-Lĕ-Tĕ

Leave me alone!

Ασε με μόνο μου! (m)

ahS-Tĕ-Mĕ MṒ-NŌ-Mᴏᴏ

Leave me alone!

Ασε με μόνη μου! (f)

ahS-Tĕ-Mĕ́ MṒ-NΕΕ-Mᴏᴏ

Go away!

Φύγε!

FΕΕ-G̲ĕ́

Be quiet!

Ησυχία!

ΕΕ-SΕΕ-ḦΕΈ-ah

That's enough!

Φτάνει!

ahR-Kĕ́-Tah́

COMMON EXPRESSIONS

When you are at a loss for words but have the feeling you should say something, try one of these!

No problem.

Κανένα πρόβλημα.

K@h-N@-N@h PR@'-VL@-M@h

Ok!

Οκέϊ!

@-K

Never mind!

Δεν πειράζει!

TH@N P@-R@h'-Z@

Very good.

πολύ καλά.

P@-L@' K@h-L@h'

Great / terrific!

Υπέροχα!

@-P@'-R@-Ḧ@h

Good luck!

Καλή τύχη!

KAH-LEE TEE-HEE

My goodness!

Θεέ μου!

THEH-EH-MOO

How beautiful!

Τι ωραία!

TEE O-REH-ah

Of course!

Βέβαια!

VEH-VEH-ah

Thats too bad!

Κρίμα!

KREE-MAH

Bravo!

Μπράβο!

BRAH-VO

USEFUL COMMANDS

Stop!

Σταμάτα!

ST@h-M@h-T@h

Go!

Πήγαινε!

PEE-Yĕ-Nĕ

Wait!

Περίμενε!

Pĕ-REE-Mĕ-Nĕ

Slow down!

Σιγά!

SEE-G@h

Come here!

Έλα εδώ!

ĕ-L@h   ĕ-THO

EMERGENCIES

Fire!

Φωτιά!

FO-TEE-ah

Help!

Βοήθεια!

VO-EE-THEE-ah

Emergency!

Έκτακτη ανάγκη!

eK-Tah-K-TEE ah-Nah-N-KEE

Call the police!

Την αστυνομία!

TEEN ah-STEE-NO-MEE-ah

Call an ambulance!

Ασθενοφόρο!

ahS-Te-NO-FO-RO

The Greece Tourism Police is staffed with foreign-language speaking personnel. They are available to provide tourist information and they work to handle tourism issues. They wear an insignia "Tourism Police" on their shirts.

ARRIVAL

Passing through customs should be easy since there are usually agents available who speak English. You may be asked how long you intend to stay and if you have anything to declare.

- Have your passport ready.

- Be sure all documents are up to date.

- Airport security conducts random baggage searches routinely. It is a good idea not to hold any item for anyone and to keep close contact with your personal items and luggage.

- While in Greece, it is wise to keep receipts for everything you buy. On leaving you will be asked to itemize your purchases as well as the amounts paid. You may be required to pay taxes on items that exceed the maximum allowance set for such purchases.

- If you have connecting flights, be sure to reconfirm in advance and arrive 2 to 3 hours early for flights and lengthy customs processing.

- Make sure your luggage is clearly marked inside and out and always keep an eye on it when in public places.

KEY WORDS

Baggage

Αποσκευές

@h-P①-SK⑥-V⑥S

Customs

Τελωνείο

T⑥-L①-N⑥-①

Passport

Διαβατήριο

TH⑥-@h-V@h-T⑥-R⑥-①

Porter

Βοηθός

V①-⑥-TH①S

Taxi

Ταξί

T@hK-S⑥

USEFUL PHRASES

Here is my passport.

Το διαβατήριο μου.

TO THEE-ah-Vah-TEE-REE-O Moo

I have nothing to declare.

Δεν έχω να δηλώσω τίποτα.

THEN E-HO TEE-PO-Tah
Nah THEE-LO-SO

I'm here on business.

Εχω έρθει για δουλειές.

E-HO ER-THEE
Yah THOO-LEE-ES

I'm on vacation.

Εχω έρθει για διακοπές.

E-HO ER-THEE Yah
THEE-ah-KO-PES

Is there a problem?

Υπάρχει κάποιο πρόβλημα;

EE PahR-HEE PRO-VLEEM-ah

PHRASEMAKER

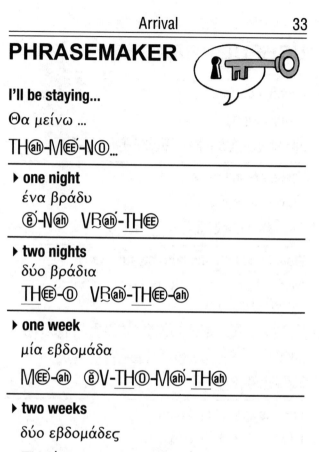

I'll be staying...

Θα μείνω ...

TH@-M€É-N©...

▶ **one night**
ένα βράδυ
@́-N@ VB@́-TH€

▶ **two nights**
δύο βράδια
TH€-© VB@́-TH€-@

▶ **one week**

μία εβδομάδα

M€́-@ @V-TH©-M@́-TH@

▶ **two weeks**

δύο εβδομάδες

TH€-© @V-TH©-M@́-TH@S

USEFUL PHRASES

I need a porter.

Χρειάζομαι βοήθεια.

ḦREE-ah̋-ZO-ME̋ VO-EE-THEE-ah̋

These are my bags.

Οι αποσκευές μου.

EE   ah̋-PO-SKE̋-VE̋S Moo

Would you help me with my luggage please?

Μποερείτε να με βοηθήσετε με τις αποσκευές μου;

BO-REE-TE̋ Nah̋ ME̋ VO-EE-THah̋-TE̋
ME̋ TEES ah̋-PO-SKE̋-VE̋S Moo
Pah̋-Rah̋-Kah̋-LŐ

I'm missing a hand bag.

Μου λείπει μία τσάντα.

Moo LEE-PEE MEE TSah̋N-Dah̋

I'm missing a suitcase.

Μου λείπει μία βαλίτσα.

Moo LEE-PEE MEE Vah̋-TEE̋S-TE̋

Thank you. This is for you.
Κρατήστε. Ευχαριστώ.

KRah̋-TEE̋S-TE̋   E̋F-H̋ah̋-REE-STŐ

PHRASEMAKER

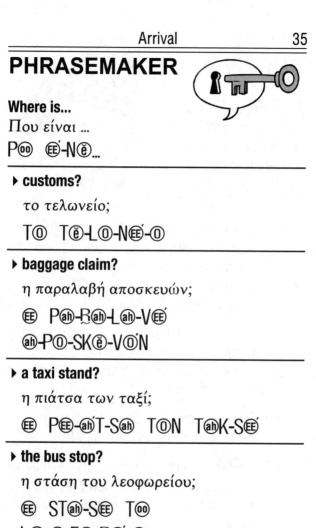

Where is...

Που είναι ...

P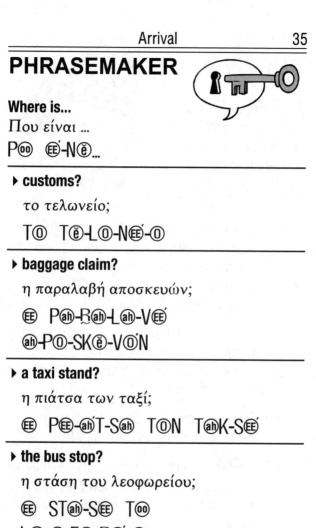⃝ EE′-N⃝...

▶ **customs?**

το τελωνείο;

T⃝ T⃝-L⃝-N⃝′-⃝

▶ **baggage claim?**

η παραλαβή αποσκευών;

EE P⃝-R⃝-L⃝-VEE′
⃝-P⃝-SK⃝-V⃝N′

▶ **a taxi stand?**

η πιάτσα των ταξί;

EE PEE′-⃝T-S⃝ T⃝N T⃝K-SEE′

▶ **the bus stop?**

η στάση του λεοφωρείου;

EE ST⃝′-SEE T⃝
L⃝-⃝-F⃝-REE′-⃝

HOTEL SURVIVAL

A wide selection of accommodations is available. Accommodations are rated by the Greek National Tourism Organization.

- The new Star Rating System begins with 5 star, 4 star, 3 star, 2, and 1. The star ratings correspond respectively with the old system as in Lux equals 5 star, A equals 4 star, B equals 3, etc.

- Make reservations well in advance and request the address of the hotel to be written in Greece as many taxi drivers do not speak English.

- Do not leave valuables or cash in your room when you are not there!

- Electrical items like blow-dryers may be provided by your hotel, however, you may want to purchase small electrical appliances there.

- It is a good idea to make sure you give your room number to persons you expect to call you. This can avoid confusion with western names.

KEY WORDS

Hotel

Ξενοδοχείο

KS**ẽ**N-**O**-TH**O**-H**ẼẼ**-**O**

Bellman

Βοηθός

V**O**-**EE**-TH**O**S

Maid

Καμαριέρα

K**ah**-M**ah**-R**EE**-Y**ẽ**-R**ah**

Message

Μήνυμα

M**ẼẼ**-N**EE**-M**ah**

Reservation

Κράτηση

KR**ah**-T**EE**-S**EE**

Room service

Υπηρεσία δωματίου

EE-P**EE**-R**ẽ**-S**EE**-**ah**   TH**O**-M**ah**-T**EE**-**oo**

CHECKING IN

My name is...

Με λένε ...

MҼ-LҼ-Nҽ...

I have a reservation.

Εχω κάνει κράτηση.

Ҽ-͋HO KӑҺ-NҼҼ KRӑҺ-TҼҼ-SҼҼ

Have you any vacancies?

Έχετε δωμάτια;

Ҽ-͋HҼ-Tҽ THO-MӑҺ-TҼҼ-ah

What is the charge per night?

Πόσο χρεώνετε τη βραδιά;

PO-SO ͋HRҼ-O-Nҽ-Tҽ
TҼҼ VBah-THҼҼ-ah

Do you have room service?

Έχετε υπηρεσια δωματιου;

Ҽ-͋HҼ-Tҽ ҼҼ-PҼҼ-Rҽ-SҼҼ-ah
THO-Mah-TҼҼ-oo

My room key, please.

Το κλειδί μου παρακαλώ.

TO KLҼҼ-THҼҼ Moo Pah-Bah-Kah-LO

PHRASEMAKER

I would like a room with...

Θα ήθελα ένα δωμάτιο με ...

THah EE-THĕ-Lah ĕ-Nah
TH̲O-Mah-TEE-O...

▶ **with a shower**

με μπάνιο

Mĕ Bah́N-YO

▶ **one bed**

μονόκλινο

MO-NO-KLEE-NO

▶ **two beds**

δίκλινο

TH̲EE-KLEE-NO

▶ **with a view**

με θέα

Mĕ THĕ-ah

USEFUL PHRASES

I would like an extra key.

Θα ήθελα ένα εξτρά κλειδί.

THⓅ ⓂⓂ-THⓇ-LⓅ Ⓡ-NⓅ

ⓇKS-TRⓅ KLⓂⓂ-THⓂⓂ

Are there any messages for me?

Έχω μυνήματα;

Ⓡ-HO MⓂⓂ-NⓂⓂ-MⓅ-TⓅ

Where is the dining room?

Που είναι η τραπεζαρία;

PⓏⓏ Ⓡ-NⓇ LⓂⓂ-TRⓅ-PⓇ-ZⓅ-RⓂⓂ-Ⓟ

Are meals included?

Με γεύματα;

MⓇ YⓇV-MⓅ-TⓅ

What time is breakfast?

Τι ώρα σερβίρετε πρωινό;

TⓂⓂ O-RⓅ SⓇR-VⓂⓂ-RⓇ-TⓇ PRO-ⓂⓂ-NO

What time is dinner?

Τι ώρα σερβίρετε βραδινό;

TⓂⓂ O-RⓅ SⓇR-VⓂⓂ-RⓇ-TⓇ

VRⓅ-THⓂⓂ-NO

PHRASEMAKER

Please wake me at...

Παρακαλώ ξυπνήστε με στις ...

Pah-Rah-Kah-LO

KSEE-NEES-Tĕ-Mĕ STEES...

▶ **6:00 AM**

έξι το πρωί

ĕKS-EE TO PRO-EE

▶ **6:30 AM**

εξίμιση το πρωί

ĕKS-EE Mĕ-SEE TO PRO-EE

▶ **7:00 AM**

επτά το πρωί

ĕP-Tah TO PRO-EE

▶ **7:30 AM**

επτά και μισή το πρωί

ĕP-Tah Mĕ-SEE TO PRO-EE

▶ **8:00 AM**

οκτώ το πρωί

OK-TO TO PRO-EE

▶ **8:30 AM**

οκτώμιση το πρωί

OK-TO ĕN Nĕ-ah TO PRO-EE

PHRASEMAKER

I need...

Χρειάζομαι ...

H̃RⒺⒺ-ⓐ-ZⓄ-Mⓔ...

▶ **a bellman**

βοηθό

VⓄ-ⒺⒺ-THⓄ́

▶ **more blankets**

περισσότερες κουβέρτες

Pⓔ-RⒺⒺ-SⓄ́-Tⓔ-Rⓔ́S   Kⓞⓞ-Vⓔ́B-Tⓔ́S

▶ **a hotel safe**

ασφαλές ξενοδοχείο

ⓐS-Fⓐ-Lⓔ́S   KSⓔ́N-Ⓞ-THⓄ-H̃ⒺⒺ́-Ⓞ

▶ **ice cubes**

παγάκια

Pⓐ-Gⓐ́-KⒺⒺ-ⓐ

▸ **a maid**

καμαριέρα

Kah-Mah-Yé-Rah

▸ **the manager**

τον διευθυντή

TON THEE-éF-THEEN-DEE

▸ **clean sheets**

καθαρά σεντόνια

Kah-THah-Rah Sé-DO-NYah

▸ **soap**

σαπούνι

Sah-Poo-NEE

▸ **toilet paper**

χαρτί υγείας

HaḧR-TEE EE-GEE-ahS

▸ **more towels**

περισσότερες πετσέτες

Pé-REE-SO-Té-RéS

PéT-Sé-TéS

PHRASEMAKER
(PROBLEMS)

There is no...

Δεν υπάρχει ...

TH**ĕ**N ㊜-P**ⓐ**R-Ḧ**㊐**...

▸ **electricity**

ρεύμα

㊜-L**ĕ**V-M**ⓐ**

▸ **heat**

θέρμανση

TH**ĕ**R-M**ⓐ**N-S**㊜**

▸ **hot water**

ζεστό νερό

Z**ĕ**S-T**ⓞ** N**ĕ**-R**ⓞ**

▸ **light**

φως

F**ⓞ**S

▸ **toilet paper**

χαρτί υγείας

Ḧ**ⓐ**R-P**㊐** ㊜-Y**㊐**-**ⓐ**S

PHRASEMAKER
(SPECIAL NEEDS)

Do you have...

Έχετε ...

ĕ-Hĕ-Tĕ...

▶ **an elevator?**

ασανσέρ;

ah-SahN-SĕR

▶ **a ramp?**

ράμπα;

RahM-Pah

▶ **a wheelchair?**

αναπηρική καρέκλα;

ah-Nah-PEE-REE-KEE Kah-Rĕ-KLah

▶ **facilities for the disabled?**

πρόσβαση αναπήρων;

PROS-Vah-SEE ah-Nah-PEE-RON

CHECKING OUT

The bill, please.

Τον λογαριασμό παρακαλώ.

TON LO-G͟ah-R-Yah-S-MO
Pah-Rah-Kah-LO

There is a mistake!

Υπάρχει κάποιο λάθος!

EE-Pah-R-HEE Kah-PEE-O Lah-THOS

Do you accept credit cards?

Δέχεστε πιστωτικές κάρτες;

THĕ-Hĕs-Tĕ
PEE-STO-TEE-Kĕs Kah-R-Tĕs

Could you have my luggage brought down?

Μπορείτε να φέρετε τις
αποσκευές μου κάτω;

BO-REE-Tĕ Nah Fĕ-Rĕ-Tĕ
TEES ah-PO-SKĕ-Vĕz-Moo
Kah-TO

Please call a taxi.

Παρακαλώ καλέστε ένα ταξί.

P@h-R@h-K@h-LO′ K@h-L@′S-T@

@′-N@h T@hK-S@

I had a very good time!

Πέρασα πολύ καλά!

P@′-R@h-S@h PO-L@ K@h-L@h′

Thanks for everything.

Ευχαριστώ για όλα.

S@hS @F-H@h-R@-STO′

Y@h O′-L@h

Good-bye.

Γειά σας.

Y@h′-S@hS

RESTAURANT SURVIVAL

Tasting Greek cuisine is a taste of long standing tradition of Greek hospitality. It is a highly revered experience when Greeks gather around the table and enjoy a meal with family and friends.

- Breakfast as a rule is rarely eaten, replaced with sweet coffee and sometimes followed by a mid-morning pastry. Lunch is usually served from 2 to 3 PM.

- Dinner is customarily eaten late in the evening between 9 and 10 PM. Some restaurants will stay open until midnight.

- You can find local fast food Souvlaki stalls or snack bars that stay open very late and into the morning hours.

- Fixed price menus or tourist menus usually provide meals at good value.

- Tavernas and Greek restaurants are relaxed and informal.

- A service charge is included in the bill; however, it is customary to leave a tip if you are satisfied with the service.

KEY WORDS

Breakfast

Πρωινό γεύμα

PRO-EE-NO YёV-Mah

Lunch

Μεσημεριανό γεύμα

Mё-SEE-Mё-R-Yah-NO YёV-Mah

Dinner

Βραδυνό γεύμα

VBah-TH-EE-NO YёV-Mah

Waiter

Σερβιτόρος

Sё-R-VEE-TO-ROS

Waitress

Σερβιτόρα

Sё-R-VEE-TO-Rah

Restaurant

Εστιατόριο

ёS-TEE-ah-TO-REE-O

USEFUL PHRASES

A table for...

Ένα τραπέζι για ...

ⓔ-Nⓐⓗ TⓇⓐⓗ-Pⓔ-ZⒺ Yⓐⓗ...

2	4
δύο	τέσσερις
TⒽⒺ-Ⓞ	Tⓔ-Sⓔ-Ⓡⓐⓗ

6

έξι

ⓔK-SⒺ

The menu, please.

Το μενού παρακαλώ.

TⓄ Mⓔ-NⓄⓄ Pⓐⓗ-Ⓡⓐⓗ-Kⓐⓗ-LⓄ

Separate checks, please.

Ξεχωριστούς λογαρισμούς παρακαλώ.

KSⓔ-HⓄ-ⓇⒺ-STⓐⓗ Pⓐⓗ-Ⓡⓐⓗ-Kⓐⓗ-LⓄ

We are in a hurry.

Βιαζόμαστε.

VⒺ-ⓐⓗ-ZⓄ-MⓐⓗS-Tⓔ

Can you recommend?

Μπορείτε να προτείνετε;

BⓄ-ⓇⒺ-Tⓔ Nⓐⓗ SⒺ-STⒺ-Sⓔ-Tⓔ

Please bring me...

Παρακαλώ μπορώ να έχω ...

Pah-Bah-Kah-LO FÖR-Tĕ Moo...

Please bring us...

Παρακαλώ μπορούμε να έχουμε ...

Pah-Bah-Kah-LO FÖR-Tĕ Mahs...

I'm hungry.	We're hungry.
Πεινάω.	Πεινάμε.
PEE-Nah-O	PEE-Nah-Mĕ

I'm thirsty.	We're thirsty.
Διψάω.	Διψάμε.
THEEP-Sah-O	THEEP-Sah—Mĕ

Is service included?

Με φιλοδώρημα;

Mĕ FEE-LO-THO-BEE-Mah

The bill, please.

Τον λογαριασμό παρακαλώ.

TON LO-Gah-BEE-ahZ-MO
Pah-Bah-Kah-LO

GREEK CUISINES AND STYLES

The basic simplicity of famous Greek Olive Oil is the secret to great Greek cuisine and is used in most dishes.

Greek food consists of the most excellent quality of fruits and vegetables. These foods are filled with aroma and full of taste and good for you to.

Add to the fresh food selections a variety of wonderful locally grown herbs and spices like oregano, thyme and rosemary and you will be swept away with an overall sense of well-being.

Appetizers (munchies) or Μεζεδες pronounced M⊙-Z⊙-TH⊙S such as octopus, olives and cheeses are usually served when you order drinks. Greek cheeses are of a wide variety and one wonderful cheese not to be missed is "feta," a crumbly white cheese.

Desserts are not usually eaten after a meal. They are normally eaten in the afternoon with a cup of coffee.

EATING ESTABLISHMENTS

Restaurants are a little more expensive but serve Greek food and a variety of foreign dishes. Try to seek out more ethnic restaurants to get a real chance to enjoy truly Greek food and its flavors!

In Greece, eating, drinking, and sharing a meal with family and friends is an important social gathering and held in the highest regard. It does not matter whether it is at home, in a restaurant, or in a taverna.

Tavernas are common eating establishments where you will find appetizers, snacks, meats, and fish.

The art of fine fresh food with a glass of wine or ouzo in a tavern framed by a picturesque Αιγαιο, ⓔ-Yⓔ-ⓞ Agean Sea is an experience unique to the country itself.

Greece is located between the Aegean Sea to the east and south and the Ionian Sea to the west in southeastern Europe and provides an excellent source of great seafood!

Fish Tavernas are found on the islands and specialize in fish and seafood cuisine.

BEVERAGE LIST

Coffee

Καφές

K@h-F@S

Decaffeinated coffee

Ντεκαφεϊνέ

D@ K@h-F@ @-N@

Tea

Τσάι

TS@h-@

Cream

Κρέμα

G@h-L@h

Sugar

Ζάχαρη

Z@h-H@h-R@

Lemon

Λεμόνι

L@-MO-N@

Milk

Γάλα

G̲ah-Lah

Hot chocolate

Ζεστή σοκολάτα

Zē-STĒ SO-KO-Lah-Tah

Juice

Χυμός

H̃EE-MOS

Orange juice

Πορτοκαλάδα (Χυμό Πορτοκάλι)

PO̲B-TO-Kah-Lah-T̲Hah

Ice water

Νερό με παγάκια

Nē-B̲O Mē Pah-G̲ah-KEE-ah

Mineral water

Μεταλικό νερό

Mē-Tah-LEE-KO Nē-B̲O

Ice

Πάγος

Pah-G̲OS

AT THE BAR

Bartender

Μπάρμαν

B@B-M@N

Drink

Ποτό

P@-T@́

With ice

Με παγάκια

M@   P@-G@-K@-@

Straight

Σκέτο

SK@́-T@

With lemon

Με λεμόνι

M@   L@-M@́-N@

PHRASEMAKER

I would like a glass of...

Μπορώ να έχω ένα ποτήρι ... παρακαλώ.

BO-RO´ N@h ë´-HO ë´-N@h

PO-TEE´-REE (...) P@h-R@h-K@h-LO´

▸ **wine**

κρασί

KR@h-SEE´

▸ **red wine**

κόκκινο κρασί

KO´-KEE-NO KR@h-SEE´

▸ **white wine**

άσπρο κρασί

@h´S-PRO KR@h´-SEE

▸ **champagne**

σαμπάνια

S@hM-P@h´N-Y@h

▸ **beer**

μπύρα

BEE´-R@h

FAMILIAR FOODS

On the following pages you will
find lists of foods you are familiar
with, along with other information
such as basic utensils and preparation
instructions.

A polite way to get a waiter's or waitress's attention
is to say "Να σας ρωτήσω …;", which means **May
I ask?**, followed by your request and thank you.

May I ask...?

Να σας ρωτήσω … ;

N@-S@'S ℝ◎-T©-S◎...

Please bring me...

Παρακαλώ μπορώ να έχω …

P@-ℝ@-K@-L◎' B◎'-ℝ◎-N@
©'-ℍ◎...

Thank you.

Ευχαριστώ.

©F-ℍ@-ℝ©-ST◎

Greek culture is firmly rooted in family, religion,
traditions, and religious feasts.

STARTERS

Appetizers

Ορεκτικά

O-REK-TEE-Kah

Bread and butter

Ψωμί με βούτυρο

PSO-MEE Ke VOO-TEE-RO

Cheese

Τυρί

TEE-REE

Fruit

Φρούτα

FROO-Tah

Salad

Σαλάτα

Sah-Lah-Tah

Soup

Σούπα

SOO-Pah

MEATS

Bacon

Μπέϊκον

BĔ́-ⒺⒺ-KⓄN

Beef

Μοσχαρίσιο κρέας

MⓄS-Hⓐʰ-RⒺⒺ́-SⒺⒺ-Ⓞ   KRĔ́-ⓐʰS

Beef steak

Μοσχαρίσια μπριζόλα

MⓄS-Hⓐʰ-RⒺⒺ́-SⒺⒺ-Ⓞ́   BRⒺⒺ-ZⓄ́-Lⓐʰ

Ham

Ζαμπόν

ZⓐʰM-BⓄ́N

Lamb

Αρνί

ⓐʰR-NⒺⒺ́

Pork

Χοιρινό

H̋ⒺⒺ-RⒺⒺ-NⓄ́

Veal

Μοσχάρι

MⓄS-Hⓐʰ́-RⒺⒺ

POULTRY

Baked chicken

Κοτόπουλο στο φούρνο

KO-TO-P∞-LO

STO F∞R-NO

Grilled chicken

Κοτόπουλο στη σχάρα

KO-TO-P∞-LO

STEE SHah-R-ah

Fried chicken

Κοτόπουλο πανέ

KO-TO-P∞-LO Pah-Ne

Turkey

Γαλοπούλα

Gah-LO-P∞-Lah

SEAFOOD

Fish

Ψάρι

PS**ah**´-R**ee**

Lobster

Αστακός

ahS-T**ah**-K**o**´S

Oysters

Στρείδια

STR**ee**´-TH**ee**-**ah**

Sardine

Σαρδέλα

S**ah**R-TH**e**´-L**ah**

Shrimp

Γαρίδες

T**ah**-R**ee**´-TH**e**S

Squid

Καλαμαράκια

K**ah**-L**ah**-M**ah**-R**ah**´K-**ee**-**ah**

Tuna

Τόνος

T**o**´-N**o**S

OTHER ENTREES

Sandwich

Σάντουϊτς

SaND-WEETS

Hot dog

Χοτ Ντογκ

HOT-DOG

Hamburger

Χάμπεργκερ

HaM-BeR-GeR

French fries

Τηγανητές πατάτες

Pah-Tah-TeS TEE-Gah-NEE-TeS

Pasta

Ζυμαρικά - Μακαρόνια

Mah-Kah-RON-Yah

Pizza

Πίτσα

PEET-Sah

VEGETABLES

Carrots

Καρότα

Kah-RŌ-Tah

Spinach

Σπανάκι

SPah-Nah-KEE

Mushrooms

Μανιτάρια

Mah-NEE-TahB-Yah

Onions

Κρεμμύδια

KBē-MEE-THĒ-ah

Potato

Πατάτα

Pah-Tah-Tah

Rice

Ρύζι

BEE-ZEE

Tomato

Τομάτα

TŌ-Mah-Tah

FRUITS

Apple

Μήλο

MEE-LO

Banana

Μπανάνα

Bah-Nah-Nah

Grapes

Σταφύλι

STah-FEE-LEE

Lemon

Λεμόνι

Lĕ-MO-NEE

Orange

Πορτοκάλι

POR-TO-Kah-LEE

Strawberry

Φράουλα

FRah-oo-Lah

Watermelon

Καρπούζι

Kah-Poo-ZEE

DESSERT

Sweets

Γλυκά

GL︎EE︎-KO︎´

Greek dessert

κανταίφι

K︎ah︎-D︎ah︎-EE︎´-F︎EE︎

Traditional cookies

κουλουράκια

K︎oo︎-L︎oo︎-B︎ah︎-K︎EE︎-ah︎

Sweet bread

τσουρέκι

TS︎oo︎-B︎e︎´-K︎EE︎

Candy

Καραμέλες

K︎ah︎-B︎ah︎-M︎e︎´-L︎e︎S

Ice cream

Παγωτό

P@-G@-T@

Ice cream cone

Χωνάκι

H@-N@-K@

Chocolate

Σοκολάτα

S@-K@-L@-T@

Strawberry

Φράουλα

FR@-@-L@

Vanilla

Βανίλια

V@-N@-LY@

CONDIMENTS

Butter

Βούτυρο

V○○́-T○○-B○

Ketchup

Κέτσαπ

K○́T-S○P

Mayonnaise

Μαγιονέζα

M○-Y○-N○́-Z○

Mustard

Μουστάρδα

M○○S-T○́B-TH○

Salt

Αλάτι

○-L○́-T○

Pepper

Πιπέρι

P○-P○́-B○

Sugar

Ζάχαρη

Z○́-H○-B○

SETTINGS

A cup

Φλιτζάνι

FLEET-Zah'-NEE

A glass

Ποτήρι

PO-TEE'-REE

A spoon

Κουτάλι

KOO-Tah'-LEE

A fork

Πηρούνι

PEE-ROO'-NEE

A knife

Μαχαίρι

Mah-HĔ'-REE

A plate

Πιάτο

Pah'-TO

A napkin

Χαρτοπετσέτα

Hah'R-PO PĔT-SĔ'-Tah

Baked

Στο φούρνο

STO FOOR-NO

Grilled

Στη σχάρα

STEE SHah-Bah

Steamed

Στον ατμό

STON ahT-MO / VBah-STO

Fried

Τηγανιτό

TEE-Gah-NEE-TO

PROBLEMS

There must be mistake.

Υπάρχει κάποιο λάθος.

EE-Pah-R-HEE Kah-PEE-O Lah-THOS

That's not what I ordered.

Δεν παρείγγηλα αυτό.

THEN Pah-REEN-GEE-Lah ahF-TO

Please check the bill.

Παρακαλώ κοιτάξτε τον λογαριασμό.

Pah-Rah-Kah-LO KEE-PahK-STe TON
LO-Gah-R-YahS-MO

PRAISE

That was a delicious meal.

Ήταν καταπληκτικό το φαγητό.

TO Fah-YEE-TO E-TahN
EE-PeR-ah-HO

GETTING AROUND

Getting around in a foreign country can be an adventure in itself! Taxi and bus drivers do not always speak English, so it is essential to be able to give simple directions. The words and phrases in this chapter will help you get where you're going.

- In Greece, taxi fees are cheap and the fares are charged by kilometer. Licensed taxis will display meters and a card listing tariffs and surcharges. Ask for the piatsa station Πιάτσα ταξί PEE-ah'T-Sah TahK-SEE.

- Taxis are allowed to pick additional passengers going to the same destination or a little before or after the final stop.

- KTEL is the intercity bus system and offers travel on the Greek mainland.

- Railways cover the mainland and connects Greece to Europe and Turkey.

- Have the address you want to go to written down in Greek.

- Remember to take a business card from your hotel to give to the taxi driver on your return.

- Carry your ID with you at all times while in Greece.

KEY WORDS

Airport

Αεροδρόμιο

@h-ĕ-ℝⓄ-THℝⓄ-Mℰ-Ⓞ

Bus Stop

Στάση λεοφωρείου

STⓐh-Sℰ Lℰ-Ⓞ-FⓄ-ℝℰ-ⓄⓄ

Taxi Stand

Πιάτσα ταξί

Pℰ-ⓐhT-Sⓐh TⓐhK-Sℰ

Train Station

Σταθμός τρένου

STⓐhTH-MⓄS Tℝℰ-NⓄⓄ

Donkeys are used on many islands for local and tourist transportation. There are ferries and boats available for transportation to outer island from mainland Greece. You can also take short flights from Athens to these islands.

AIR TRAVEL

A one-way ticket, please.

Ένα απλό εισιτήριο παρακαλώ.

Ĕ-Nah ah-P-LO EE-SEE-TEE-REE-O
Pah-Rah-Kah-LO

A round-trip ticket.

Ένα εισιτήριο με επιστροφή παρακαλώ.

Ĕ-Nah EE-SEE-TEE-REE-O
Mĕ ĕ-PEES-TRO-FEE
Pah-Rah-Kah-LO

First class

Πρώτη θέση

PRO-TEE ĕ-SEE

How much do I owe?

Τι σας οφείλω;

TEE O-FEE-LO Pah-Rah-Kah-LO

The gate

Θύρα (Πύλη)

THEE-Rah

PHRASEMAKER

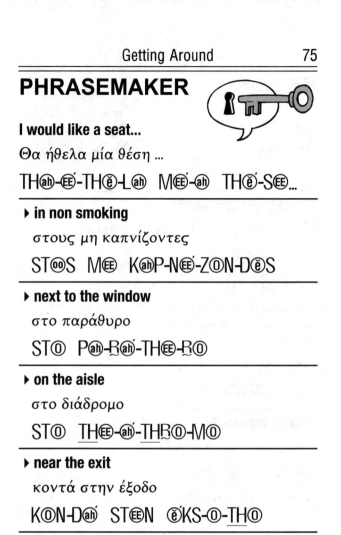

I would like a seat...

Θα ήθελα μία θέση ...

TH@-EE-TH@-L@h M@-@h TH@-S@...

▸ **in non smoking**

στους μη καπνίζοντες

ST@S M@ K@P-N@-Z@N-D@S

▸ **next to the window**

στο παράθυρο

ST@ P@-R@-TH@-R@

▸ **on the aisle**

στο διάδρομο

ST@ TH@-@h-THR@-M@

▸ **near the exit**

κοντά στην έξοδο

K@N-D@h ST@N @KS-@-TH@

I would like a ticket in first class.

Θα ήθελα ένα εισητήριο στην πρώτη θέση.

TH@ @-TH@-L@h @-N@h

@-S@-T@-R@-@ ST@N

PR@-T@ TH@-S@

BY BUS

Bus

Λεωφορείο

L**ĕ**-**O**-F**O**-R**EE**-**O**

Where is the bus stop?

Που είναι η στάση του λεωφορείου;

P**oo** **EE**-N**ĕ** **EE**

ST**ah**-S**EE** T**oo**

L**ĕ**-**O**-F**O**-R**EE**-**oo**

Do you go to...?

Πηγαίνετε ... ;

P**EE**-Y**ĕ**N-**ĕ**-T**ĕ**...

What is the fare?

Πόσο κάνει το εισητήριο;

P**O**-S**O** K**ah**-N**EE** T**O**

EE-S**EE**-T**EE**-R**EE**-**O**

PHRASEMAKER

Which bus goes to...

Ποιό λεωφορείο πηγαίνει ...

PEE-O′ LĔ-O-FO-RĔE-O PEE-YĔ-NEE...

▸ **the beach?**

στην παραλία;

STEEN Pah-Rah-LEE-ah′

▸ **the market?**

στην αγορά;

STEEN ah-GO-Rah′

▸ **the airport?**

στο αεροδρόμιο;

STO ah-ĕ-RO-THRO′-MEE-O

▸ **the train station?**

στον σταθμό του τρένου;

STON STah TH-MO′ TOO TRĔ-NOO

BY CAR

Can you help me?

Μπορείτε να με βοηθήσετε
παρακαλώ;

BO-REE-Tĕ Nah Mĕ
Voʊ-THEE-Sĕ-TEE Pah-Rah-Kah-LO

My car won't start. (Lit. My engine will not start.)

Δεν παίρνει μπρος η μηχανή.

THĕN PĕR-NEE BROS EE
MEE-Hah-NEE

Can you fix it?

Μπορείτε να την φτιάξετε;

BO-REE-Tĕ Nah TO
FTEE-ahKS-ĕ-Tĕ

What will it cost?

Πόσο θα κοστίσει;

PO-SO THah KO-STEE-SEE

How long will it take?

Πόσο χρόνο θα πάρει;

PO-SEE HRO-NO THah Pah-REE

PHRASEMAKER

Please check...

Παρακαλώ κοιτάξτε ...

P@ɦ-B@ɦ-K@ɦ-LO
K©-T@ɦKS-T©...

▸ **the battery**

την μπαταρία

T©N B@ɦ-T@ɦ-B©-@ɦ

▸ **the brakes**

τα φρένα

T@ɦ FB©-N@ɦ

▸ **the oil**

τα λάδια

T@ɦ L@ɦ-TH©-@ɦ

▸ **the tires**

τα λάστιχα

T@ɦ L@ɦS-T©-K@ɦ

▸ **the water**

το νερό

TO N©-BO

SUBWAYS AND TRAINS

Where is the train station?

Που είναι ο σταθμός του τρένου;

P◎ ℰ-Nℰ ◎ ST⒜TH-M◎S
T◎ TRℰ-N◎

A one-way ticket, please.

Ένα εισητήριο απλό παρακαλώ.

ℰ-N⒜ M◎-N◎ ℰ-Sℰ-Tℰ-Rℰ-◎
P⒜-R⒜-K⒜-L◎

A round trip ticket, please.

Ένα εισιτήριο με επιστροφή παρακαλώ.

ℰ-N⒜ ℰ-Sℰ-Tℰ-Rℰ-◎ Mℰ
ℰ-PℰS-TR◎-Fℰ P⒜-R⒜-K⒜-L◎

First class

Πρώτη θέση

PR◎-Tℰ THℰ-Sℰ

Second class

Δεύτερη θέση

THℰF-Tℰ-Rℰ THℰ-Sℰ

What is the fare?

Πόσο έχει το εισιτήριο;

PŌ'-SŌ KⒶ'-NⒺⒺ TŌ
ⒺⒺ-SⒺⒺ-TⒺⒺ-RⒺⒺ-Ō

Is this seat taken?

Είναι πιασμένη η θέση;

ⒺⒺ-NĔ PⒺⒺ-ⒶS-MĔ'-NⒺⒺ
ⒺⒺ THĔ'-SⒺⒺ

Do I have to change trains?

Θα αλλάξω τρένα;

THⒶ Ⓐ-LⒶ'KS-Ō TRĔ'-NⒶ

Where are we?

Που βρισκόμαστε;

PⓄⓄ VRⒺⒺ-SKŌ'-MⒶS-TĔ

BY TAXI

Please call a taxi for me.

Καλέστε ένα ταξί παρακαλώ.

P@h-R@h-K@h-L⓪́ K@h-L@̆́S-T@̆

@̆-N@h T@hK-S@€

Are you available?

Ελεύθερος;

@̆-L@̆F-TH@̆-R⓪́S

I want to go...

Θέλω να πάω ...

TH@̆́-L⓪ N@h-P@h-⓪...

Stop here, please.

Σταματήστε εδώ παρακαλώ.

ST@h-M@h-T@€́S-T@̆ @̆-TH⓪́

P@h-R@h-K@h-L⓪́

Please wait.

Περιμένετε παρακαλώ.

P@̆-R@€-M@̆́-N@̆-T@̆ P@h-R@h-K@h-L⓪́

How much do I owe?

Τι οφείλω;

T@€ S@hS ⓪-F@€́-L⓪

PHRASEMAKER

The simplest way to get to
where you want to go is to
name the destination and say **please**.

▶ **This address...**

Σε αυτή τη διεύθυνση ...

S@ @F-T@ T@
TH@-@F-TH@N-S@

Have someone at your hotel write down the address
for you in Greek.

▶ **This hotel...**

Σε αυτό το ξενοδοχείο ...

@F-T@ T@ KS@N-@-TH@-H@-@

▶ **Airport...**

Στο αεροδρόμιο ...

ST@ @-@-R@-TH@-M@-@

▶ **Subway station...**

Στάση μετρό ...

ST@-S@ M@-TR@

...please.

... παρακαλώ.

..P@-R@-K@-L@

SHOPPING

Whether you plan a major shopping spree or just need to purchase some basic necessities, the following information is useful.

- Upon arriving in Greece, tourists must fill out a customs declaration form. Keep this with you until you leave as it lists your personal items.

- Visitors to Greece will enjoy shopping in the Kolonaki and Plaka. Ermou, one of the most famous streets for shopping, is located at Plaka.

- Kolonaki offers upscale shopping and is a wonderful district.

- Thessaloniki offers additional big city shopping, much like Athens. You will find one of the best food markets here too!

- There is something for everyone and every budget from souvenirs to antiques.

- Every island offers a plethora of shopping delights. Santorini is known for its distinctly flavorful wines, Crete for beautifully woven rugs and Rhodes for leather goods.

- So, enjoy and remember to keep all your shopping receipts.

KEY WORDS

Credit card

Πιστωτική κάρτα

PⒺⒺ-STⓄ-TⒺⒺ-ⓀⒺⒺ́ KⓐⓗⒽ-Tⓐⓗ

Money

Χρήματα / Λεφτά

H̃RⒺⒺ́-Mⓐⓗ-Tⓐⓗ / Lⓔ̃F-Tⓐⓗ́

Receipt

Απόδειξη

ⓐⓗ-PⓄ́-THⒺⒺK-SⒺⒺ

Sale

Έκπτωση

PⓄ́-LⒺⒺ-SⒺⒺ

Store

Κατάστημα

Kⓐⓗ-Tⓐⓗ́S-TⒺⒺ-Mⓐⓗ

Traveler's check

Ταξιδιωτικές επιταγές

TⓐⓗK-SⒺⒺ-TH-ⒺⒺ-Ⓞ-TⒺⒺ-ⓀⒺⒺ́S
ⓔ̃-PⒺⒺ-Tⓐⓗ-Yⓔ̃́S

USEFUL PHRASES

Do you have...?

Έχετε ... ;

ĕ-H́ĕ-Tĕ...

I'm looking for...

Ψάχνω ...

PSah-H́No...

How much does it cost?

Πόσο κάνει;

PO-SO Kah-NEE /

PO-SO KOS-TEE-ZEE

When do the shops open?

Πότε ανοίγουν τα μαγαζιά;

PO-Tĕ ah-NEE-GooN

Tah Mah-Gah-ZEE-ah

When do the shops close?

Πότε κλείνουν τα μαγαζιά;

PO-Tĕ KLEE-NooN

Tah Mah-Gah-ZEE-ah

No, thank you.

Όχι, ευχαριστώ.

Ⓞ-ḦⒺ ⓔF-Ḧⓐ-ⓇⒺ-STⓄ

I´m just looking.

Κοιτάζω.

ⓐ-PLⓐ KⒺ-Tⓐ-ZⓄ

That's too expensive.

Είναι πολύ ακριβό.

Ⓔ-Nⓔ PⓄ-LⒺ ⓐ-KⓇⒺ-VⓄ

Can't you give me a discount?

Μπορείτε να κάνετε έκπτωση;

ḄⓄ-ḄⒺ-Tⓔ Nⓐ Kⓐ-Nⓔ-Tⓔ
ⓔK-PTⓄ-SⒺ

I'll take it.

Θα το πάρω.

THⓐ TⓄ Pⓐ-ḄⓄ

I'd like a receipt, please.

Θα ήθελα απόδειξη παρακαλώ.

THⓐ Ⓔ-THⓔ-Lⓐ
ⓐ-PⓄ-THⒺK-SⒺ
Pⓐ-Ḅⓐ-Kⓐ-LⓄ

SHOPS AND SERVICES

Bakery

Φούρνος

FⓄB-NⓄS

Bank

Τράπεζα

TRⓐ-Pⓔ-Zⓐ

Hair salon

Κομμωτήριο

KⓄ-MⓄ-TⒺ-BⒺ-Ⓞ

Barbershop

Κουρείο

KⓄⓄ-BⒺ-Ⓞ

Jewelry store

Κοσμηματοπωλείο

KⓄ-SMⒺ-Mⓐ-TⓄ-PⓄ-LⒺ-Ⓞ

Bookstore

Βιβλιοπωλείο

VⒺ-VLⒺ-Ⓞ-PⓄ-LⒺ-Ⓞ

News stand

Περίπτερο

Pⓔ-BⒺP-Tⓔ-BⓄ

Camera shop

Κατάστημα με κάμερες

Kⓐ-TⓐS-TⒺ-Mⓐ

Mⓔ Kⓐ-Mⓔ-BⓔS

Pharmacy

Φαρμακείο

FⓐB-Mⓐ-KⒺ-Ⓞ

SHOPPING LIST

On the following pages you will find some common items you may need to purchase on your trip.

Aspirin

Ασπιρίνη

ⓐⓗS-Pⓔⓔ-Rⓔⓔ-Nⓔⓔ

Cigarettes

Τσιγάρα

TSⓔⓔ-Gⓐⓗ-Rⓐⓗ

Deodorant

Αποσμητικό

ⓐⓗ-Pⓞⓢ-Mⓔⓔ-Tⓔⓔ-Kⓞ́

Dress

Φόρεμα

Fⓞ́-Rⓔ̃-Mⓐⓗ

Film (camera)

Φιλμ

FⓔⓔLM

Perfume
Άρωμα

ah-RO-Mah

Razor blades
Ξυραφάκι

KSEE-Bah-Fah-KEE

Shampoo
Σαμπουάν

SahM-Poo-ahN

Shaving cream (foam)
Αφρός ξυρίσματος

ah-FBOS KSEE-BEE-SMah-TOS

Shirt
Πουκάμισο

Poo-Kah-MEE-SO

Sunglasses
Γυαλιά ηλίου

Yah L-Yah EE-LEE-oo

Suntan oil

Αντηλιακό

@ñ-D@-L@-@ñ-K①

Toothbrush

Οδοντόβουρτσα

①-T̲H̲①N-D①-V⑩B-TS@ñ

Toothpaste

Οδοντόκρεμα

①-T̲H̲①N-D①-KB@-M@ñ

Water (bottled)

Εμφιαλωμένο νερό

@M-F@-@ñ-L①-M@-N① N@-B①

Water (mineral)

Μεταλλικό νερό

M@-T@ñ-L@-K① N@-B①

ESSENTIAL SERVICES

THE BANK

As a traveler in a foreign country your primary contact with banks will be to exchange money.

- The official Greek currency is the euro which is the same throughout the euro countries. Banknotes are in the following demoniations, 5, 10, 20, 50, 100, 200, and 500. Cents are 1, 2, 5, 10, 50 cents, and 1 and 2 euro.

- Banks are usually open from Mondays to Fridays between 9 AM and 2 PM.

- Currency can be changed at the airport in convenient machines as well as banks and official exchanges shops.

- ATMs are available in small towns, but there may be only one and they are limited in how much they dispense.

- Most large hotels and tourist areas accept major credit cards, however, this may not be the case in the smaller towns.

- Credit cards are accepted; however, keep in mind that there will be a fee for the conversion to pay in euro.

KEY WORDS

Bank

Τράπεζα

TRah-Pĕ-Zah

Exchange office

Πρακτορείο συναλλάγματος

PRah-K-TO-REE-O

SEE-Nah-Lahg-Mah-TOS

Money

λεφτά / χρήματα

LĕF-Tah / HREE-Mah-Tah

Exchange rate

Τιμή συναλλάγματος

TEE-MEE

SEE-Nah-Lahg-Mah-TOS

Traveler's check

Ταξιδιωτική επιταγή

Tah-K-SEE-THEE-O-TEE-KEE

ĕ-PEE-Tah-YEE

USEFUL PHRASES

Where is the bank?

Που είναι η τράπεζα;

P🔘🔘 🔘🔘-N🔘 🔘🔘 TR🔘-P🔘-Z🔘

At what time does the bank open?

Τι ώρα ανοίγει η τράπεζα;

T🔘🔘 🔘'-R🔘 🔘-N🔘🔘-Y🔘

🔘🔘 TR🔘-P🔘-Z🔘

Where is the exchange office?

Πού είναι το πρακτορείο
συναλλάγματος;

P🔘🔘 🔘🔘-N🔘 T🔘

PR🔘-KT🔘-R🔘🔘-🔘

S🔘🔘N-🔘-L🔘G-M🔘-T🔘S

At what time does the exchange office open?

Τι ώρα ανοίγει το πρακτορείο
συναλλάγματος;

T🔘🔘 🔘'-R🔘 🔘-N🔘🔘-Y🔘

T🔘 PR🔘-KT🔘-R🔘🔘-🔘

S🔘🔘N-🔘-L🔘G-M🔘-T🔘S

Can I change dollars here?

Μπορώ να αλλάξω
δολάρια εδώ;

BO-RÓ Nah ah-Lah-KSO
THO-Lah-REE-ah e-THÓ

What is the exchange rate?

Ποια είναι η τιμή
συναλλάγματος;

PEE-ah EE-Ne
EE ah-GO-Rah
SEEN-ah-Lah-Gah-Mah-TOS

I need change.

Χρειάζομαι ψιλά.

HREE-ah-ZO-Me PSE-Lah

Do you have an ATM?

Έχετε μηχάνημα τραπέζης;

e-He-Te
MEE-Hah-NEE-Mah
TRah-Pe-ZEES

POST OFFICE

If you are planning on sending letters and postcards, be sure to send them early so that you don't arrive home before they do.

KEY WORDS

Air mail

Αεροπορικώς

ah-ĕ-RO-PO-REE-KO'S

Letter

Γράμμα

GRah'-Mah

Post office

Ταχυδρομείο

Tah-HEE-THRO-MEE-O

Postcard

καρτ-ποστάλ

KahRT POS-Tah'L

Stamp

Γραμματόσημο

GRah-Mah-TO'-SEE-MO

USEFUL PHRASES

Where is the post office?

Πού είναι το ταχυδρομείο;

Poo EE-Nĕ TO Tah-HEE-THRO-MEE-o

What time does the post office open?

Τι ώρα ανοίγει το ταχυδρομείο;

TEE O'-Rah ah-NEE-YEE TO
Tah-HEE-THRO-MEE-o

I need...

Χρειάζομαι ...

HREE-ah'-ZO-Mĕ...

I need stamps.

Χρειάζομαι γραμματόσημα.

HREE-ah'-ZO-Mĕ
GRah-Mah-TO'-SEE-Mah

I need envelopes.

Χρειάζομαι φακέλους.

HREE-ah'-ZO-Mĕ Fah-KĕE-LOS

I need a pen.

Χρειάζομαι ένα στιλό.

HREE-ah'-ZO-Mĕ ĕ-Nah STEE-LO'

TELEPHONE

Placing phone calls in Greece can be
a test of will and stamina! Besides
the obvious language barriers, service
can vary greatly from one city to the
next.

- You can purchase pay-as-you-go cell
  phones and add units as needed.

- You can purchase a prepaid internet
  access card from a Periptero which will
  allow you to access your e-mail and surf
  the net. Look for the yellow kiosks to
  purchase internet access cards.

- Upscale hotels offer online connections
  and WiFi services but they are not always
  reliable.

- Internet cafés offer reliable services along
  with great coffee as well as the chance
  to interact with locals. The downside
  is that they will charge more to get
  connected; however, in terms of reliability,
  accessibility, and faster connections, in
  most cases it is worth it.

- Internet cafés are quite popular and you
  may find them in hotels and tavernas.

KEY WORDS

Information

Πληροφορίες

PLEE-RO-FO-REE-ěS

Long distance call

Υπεραστικό

EE-Pě-RahS-TEE-KO

Phone book

Τηλεφωνικός κατάλογος

TEE-Lě-FO-NEE-KOS
Kah-Tah-LO-GOS

Public telephone

Καρτοτηλέφωνο

KahR-TO-TEE-Lě-FO-NO

Telephone

Τηλέφωνο

TEE-Lě-FO-NO

USEFUL PHRASES

Where is the telephone?

Που είναι το τηλέφωνο;

P◎◎ ㏇-N⒠

T◎ T㏌-L⒠-F◎-N◎

Where is the public telephone?

Πού είναι το καρτοτηλέφωνο;

P◎◎ ㏇-N⒠ T◎

K⒜B-T◎-T㏌-L⒠-F◎-N◎

May I use your telephone?

Μπορώ να κάνω
ένα τηλεφώνημα;

B◎-B◎´ N⒜

H´B㏌-S㏌-M◎-P㏌-S◎

T◎ T㏌-L⒠-F◎-N◎´-S⒜S

I want to call this number...

Θελω να καλεσω αυτον τον αριθμο...

THĔ-LO Nah Kah-LĔ-SO ahF-TON
TON ah-REETH-MO...

SIGHTSEEING AND ENTERTAINMENT

Mykonos and Santorini offer great party cruises in the summertime!

Greek Islands

Santorini

Σαντορίνη

S@N-T@-R@-N@

Corfu K@R-F@

Κέρκυρα

K@R-K@-R@

Mykonos

Μύκονος

M@-K@-N@S

Crete

Κρήτη

KR@-T@

Rhodes

Ρόδος

R@-D@S

Paros

Πάρος

P@-R@S

Acropolis

Ακρόπολη

@-KR@-P@-L@

Plaka

Πλάκα

PL@-K@

Parthenon

Παρθενώνας

P@R-TH@-N@-N@S

Syntagma Square

Σύνταγμα

S@N-D@G-M@

KEY WORDS

Admission price

Τιμή εισόδου

T㉞-M㉞́ ㉞-S㋵́-T̲H̲⓪⓪

Map

Χάρτης

H⒜B-T㉞S

Reservation

Κράτηση

KB⒜́-T㉞-S㉞

Ticket

Εισιτήριο

㉞-S㉞-T㉞́-B㉞-⓪

Tour

Τουρ

T⓪⓪B

Tour guide

Ξεναγός

KS㉞N-⒜-G㋵́S

USEFUL PHRASES

Where is the tourist agency?

Που είναι το τουριστικό γραφείο;

P㏇ ㎢-N㏂ T㏒
T㏒-R㏝S-T㏝-K㏒ GR㏂-F㏝-㏒

Where do I buy a ticket?

Που μπορώ να αγοράσω εισιτήριο;

P㏇ B㏒-R㏒ N㏂ ㏂-G㏒-B㏂-S㏒
㎢-S㏝-T㏝-R㏝-㏒

How much?

Πόσο κοστίζει;

P㏒-S㏒ K㏂-N㏝

How long?

Πόσες ώρες κάνει;

P㏒-S㏝S ㏒-R㏝S K㏂-N㏝

When?

Πότε;

P㏒-T㏂

Where?

Που;

P㏇

Do I need reservations?

Χρειάζομαι κράτηση;

ḦRͤͤ-a̍h-Z⓪-Mͤ̄ KRa̍h-Tͤͤ-Sͤͤ

Does the guide speak English?

Ο ξεναγός μιλάει αγγλικά;

⓪ KSͤ̄N-a̍h-G⓪́S
Mͤͤ-La̍h-ͤͤ a̍hN-GLͤͤ-Ka̍h

How much do children pay?

Πόσο κάνει το παιδικό εισιτήριο;

P⓪́-S⓪ Ka̍h-Nͤͤ Pͤ̄-THͤͤ-K⓪́
ͤͤ-Sͤͤ-Tͤ̄Ṟ-ͤͤ-⓪

I need your help.

Χρειάζομαι βοήθεια.

ḦRͤͤ-a̍h-Z⓪-Mͤ̄
V⓪-ͤ́ͤ-THͤͤ-a̍h

Thank you.

Ευχαριστώ.

ͤ̄F-Ḧa̍h-Ṟͤͤ-ST⓪́

PHRASEMAKER

May I invite you to...

να σας καλέσω ...

N@-S@S K@-L@-S@...

▶ **a concert?**

στη συναυλία;

ST@ S@-N@-VL@-@

▶ **dance?**

να πάμε να χορέψουμε;

N@ P@-M@ N@ H@-R@-PS@-M@

▶ **dinner?**

για βραδυνό γεύμα;

Y@ VR@-TH@-N@ Y@V-M@

▶ **the movies?**

να πάμε σινεμά;

N@ P@-M@ S@N-@-M@

▶ **the theater?**

να πάμε στο θέατρο;

N@ P@-M@ ST@ TH@-@-TR@

PHRASEMAKER

Where can I find...

Που μπορώ να βρω ...

P⊙⊙ B⊙-R⊙́ N@h VR⊙́...

▸ **a gym?**

γυμναστήριο;

Y☉M-N@hS-T☉R-☉-⊙

▸ **a swimming pool?**

πισίνα;

P☉-S☉́-N@h

▸ **a tennis court?**

γήπεδο του τέννις;

Y☉-P☉́-TH⊙ T⊙⊙ T☉́-N☉S

▸ **a golf course?**

γήπεδο του γκολφ;

Y☉́-P☉́-TH⊙ T⊙⊙ G⊙LF

HEALTH

Hopefully you will not need medical attention on your trip. If you do, it is important to communicate basic information regarding your condition.

- Travelers to Greece are urged to obtain overseas medical insurance which includes hospitalization and medical evacuation.

- If you take prescription medicine, carry your prescription with you in original containers.

- Take a small first-aid kit with you. You may want to include basic cold, anti-diarrhea, and allergy medications. However, you should be able to find most items, like aspirin, locally.

- City hospitals and emergency clinics are located on mainland Greece. Small towns have medical centers. Medical care is run under socialized medicine and you can be referred to a doctor by local pharmacies.

- A "Green Cross" indicates a pharmacy. Pharmacies can handle small medical needs such and first-aid. For after hour needs, there is a pharmacy that is designated to stay open all night.

KEY WORDS

Ambulance

Ασθενοφόρο

@S-TH®N-O-FO-RO

Dentist

Οδοντίατρος

O-THON-DEE-@-TROS

Doctor

Γιατρός

Y@-TROS

Hospital

Νοσοκομείο

NO-SO-KO-MEE-O

Prescription

Συνταγή

SEE-D@-YEE

USEFUL PHRASES

I am sick. (m)

Είμαι άρρωστος.

EE-ME ah-RO-STOS

I am sick. (f)

Είμαι άρρωστη.

EE-ME ah-RO-STEE

My child is sick.

Το παιδί μου είναι άρρωστο.

TO PE-THEE Moo EE-NE
ah-RO-STO

I need a doctor.

Χρειάζομαι γιατρό.

HREE-ah-ZO-ME Yah-TRO

It's an emergency!

Είναι επείγον!

EE-NE EK-Tah-K-TEE ah-NahN-GEE

Call an ambulance!

Καλέστε ασθενοφόρο!

Kah-LES-TE TO ah-STE-NO-FO-RO

I'm allergic to...

Είμαι αλλεργικός στο ... (m)

EE-MĔ ah-L ĔR-YEE-KOS...

Είμαι αλλεργική στο ... (f)

EE-MĔ ah-L ĔR-YEE-KEE...

I'm pregnant.

Είμαι έγκυος.

EE-MĔ ĔN-KEE-OS

I'm diabetic.

Είμαι διαβητικός. (m)

EE-MĔ THEE ah-VEE-TEE-KOS

Είμαι διαβητική. (f)

EE-MĔ THEE ah-VEE-TEE-KEE

I have a heart condition.

Έχω την καρδιά μου.

Ĕ-HO TEEN Kah R-THEE-ah MOO

I have high blood pressure.

Έχω πίεση.

Ĕ-HO PEE-ĕ-SEE

I have low blood pressure.

Έχω υπόταση.

Ĕ-HO EE-PO-Tĕ-SEE

PHRASEMAKER

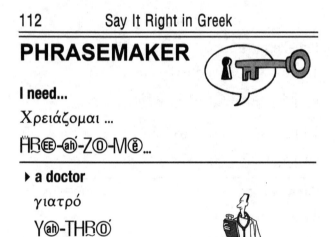

I need...

Χρειάζομαι ...

ḦRÊE-ah́-ZO-Mễ...

▶ **a doctor**

γιατρό

Y@h-THRO´

▶ **a dentist**

οδοντίατρο

O-TH̲ON-DÊE-@h-TRO

▶ **an eye doctor**

οφθαλμίατρο

OF-TH@hL-MÊE-@h-TRO

▶ **a nurse**

νοσοκόμα

NO-SO-KO´-M@h

▶ **a pharmacy**

φαρμακείο

F@hR-M@h-KÊE-O

PHRASEMAKER
(AT THE PHARMACY)

Do you have...

Έχετε ...

Ĕ́-HĔ-TĔ...

▶ **aspirin?**

ασπιρίνη;

ah-SPEE-REE-NEE

▶ **Band-Aids?**

χανζαπλάστ;

HahN-ZO-PLahST

▶ **cough syrup?**

σιρόπι για το βήχα;

SEE-RO-PEE Yah TO VEE-Hah

▶ **ear drops?**

σταγόνες για τα αυτιά;

STah-GO-NĔS Yah Tah ahF-TEE-ah

BUSINESS TRAVEL

It is important to show appreciation and interest in another person's language and culture, particularly when doing business. A few well-pronounced phrases can make a great impression.

- Business cards are essential. If possible, ensure that the information is printed in English and Greek. Present the Greek side up to the recipient.

- Be sure to make appointment in advance and to be on time for your meeting.

- Business dress is conservative and dark colors are in good taste.

- Respect is given to those of seniority and their opinions count.

- The handshake is the preferred form of greeting.

- Initially meetings may begin laid back; however, be ready and inspired for a vibrant discussion of the issues and be prepared to answer many questions.

- It is a good idea to take pains in developing the business relationship. It is never accepted well to act casual with your business counterpart when there is no relationship base.

- Do not use the "OK" sign as it is considered very rude.

KEY WORDS

Appointment

Ραντεβού

RahN-Dē-Voo

Business card

Κάρτα

KahR-Tah

Meeting

Σύσκεψη

SEE-SKē-PSEE

Office

Γραφείο

GRah-FEE-O

Presentation

Παρουσίαση

Pah-Roo-SEE-ah-SEE

Telephone

Τηλέφωνο

TEE-Lē-FO-NO

USEFUL PHRASES

I have an appointment.

Έχω ραντεβού.

ⓔ-ḦⓄ   ⓔ-Nⓐⓗ   RⓐⓗN-Dⓔ-Vⓞⓞ

(Say your name first and follow with)
...Pleased to meet you.

... Χαίρω πολύ.

...Ḧⓔ-RⓄ   PⓄ-Lⓔⓔ

Here is my card.

Η κάρτα μου.

ⓔⓔ   KⓐⓗR-Tⓐⓗ   Mⓞⓞ

I need an interpreter.

Χρειάζομαι διερμηνέα.

ḦRⓔⓔ-ⓐⓗ-ZⓄ-Mⓔ

THⓔⓔ-ⓔR-Mⓔⓔ-Nⓔ-ⓐⓗ

Many Greeks speak English but it may be good idea to bring
your own interpreter.

Can you write your address for me?

Μπορείτε να γράψετε τη διεύθυνσή σας;

MOO GRah-PSe-Te TeN
THEE-eF-THeN-See SahS

Can you write your phone number?

Μπορείτε να γράψετε το τηλέφωνό σας;

BO-REE-Te Nah GRah-PSe-Te
TO TEE-Le-FO NO-SahS

This is my phone number.

Αυτό είναι το τηλέφωνό μου.

ahF-TO EE-Ne TO
TEE-Le-FO-NO MOO

His name is...

Τον λένε ...

TON Le-Ne

Her name is...

Την λένε ...

TeN Le-Ne

Good-bye

Γειά σας

Yah-SahS

PHRASEMAKER

I need...

Χρειάζομαι ...

HREE-ah-ZO-ME...

▶ **a computer**

έναν υπολογιστή

EE-PO-LO-YEE-STEE

▶ **a copy machine**

φωτοτυπικό μηχάνημα

FO-TO-TEE-PEE-KO
MEE-Hah-NEE-Mah

▶ **a fax**

να στείλω ένα φαξ

FahKS

▶ **a lawyer**

δικηγόρο

THEE-KEE-GO-RO

▶ **conference room**

αίθουσα σύσκεψης

ĕ́-TH⊚⊚-S⒜   SEES-KĕP-SEES

▶ **a pen**

στυλό

STEE-LO͠

▶ **stamps**

γραμματόσημα

GR⒜-M⒜-TO͠-SEE-M⒜

GENERAL INFORMATION

SEASONS

Spring

Άνοιξη

@ĥ-N@-KS@

Summer

Καλοκαίρι

K@-L@-K@-R@

Autumn

Φθινόπωρο

FTH@-N@-P@-R@

Winter

Χειμώνας

H@-M@-N@S

THE DAYS

Monday

Δευτέρα

TH(ĕ)F-T(ĕ́)-R(ah)

Tuesday

Τρίτη

TR(EE)-T(EE)

Wednesday

Τετάρτη

T(ĕ)-T(ah)R-T(EE)

Thursday

Πέμπτη

P(ĕ́)MP-T(EE)

Friday

Παρασκευή

P(ah)-R(ah)-SK(ĕ)-V(EÉ)

Saturday

Σάββατο

S(ah́)-V(ah)-T(O)

Sunday

Κυριακή

K(EE)-R(EE)-(ah)-K(EÉ)

THE MONTHS

January	February
Ιανουάριος	Φεβρουάριος.
EE-ah-N00-ah-REE-OS	FēV-R00-ah-REE-OS

March	April
Μάρτιος	Απρίλιος
MahR-TEE-OS	ah-PREE-LEE-OS

May	June
Μάιος	Ιούνιος
Mahi-EE-OS	EE-oo-NEE-OS

July	August
Ιούλιος	Αύγουστος
EE-oo-LEE-OS	ahV-G00-STOS

September	October
Σεπτέμβριος	Οκτώβριος
SēP-TēM-VREE-OS	OK-TO-VREE-OS

November	December
Νοέμβριος	Δεκέμβριος
NO-ēM-VREE-OS	THē-KēM-VREE-OS

COLORS

Black	**White**
Μαύρο	Άσπρο
MOV-RO	ahS-PRO

Blue	**Brown**
Μπλε	Καφέ
BLё	Kah-Fё

Gray	**Gold**
Γκρι	Χρυσό
GREE	HREE-SO

Orange	**Yellow**
Πορτοκαλί	Κίτρινο
POR-TO-Kah-LEE	KEE-TREE-NO

Red	**Green**
Κόκκινο	Πράσινο
KO-KEE-NO	PRah-SEE-NO

Pink	**Purple**
Ροζ	Μωβ
ROZ	MOV

NUMBERS

0	1	2
Μηδέν	Ένα	Δύο
MEE-THEN	e-Nah	THEE-O

3	4	5	6
Τρία	Τέσσερα	Πέντε	Έξι
TREE-ah	Te-Se-Bah	PeN-De	eK-SEE

7	8	9	10
Επτά	Οκτώ	Εννέα	Δέκα
eP-Tah'K	OK-TO	e-Ne-ah	THe-Kah

11	12
Έντεκα	Δώδεκα
eN-De-Kah	THO-THe-Kah

13	14
Δέκατρία	Δεκατέσσερα
THe-Kah-TREE-ah	THe-Kah-Te-Se-Bah

15	16
Δεκαπέντε	Δεκαέξι
THe-Kah-PeN-De	THe-Kah-e-KSEE

17	18
Δεκαεπτά	Δεκαοκτώ
THe-Kah-eP-Tah	THe-Kah-OK-TO

19	20
Δεκαεννέα	Είκοσι
TH`ĕ`-K`ah`-`ĕ`-N`ĕ`-`ah`	`ĒĒ`-K`O`-S`ĒĒ`

30	40
Τριάντα	Σαράντα
TR`ĒĒ`-`ah`N-D`ah`	S`ah`-R`ah`N-D`ah`

50	60
Πενήντα	Εξήντα
P`ĕ`-N`ĒĒ`N-D`ah`	`ĕ`K-S`ĒĒ`N-D`ah`

70	80
Εβδομήντα	Ογδόντα
`ĕ`V-TH`O`-M`ĒĒ`N-D`ah`	`O`G-TH`O`N-D`ah`

90	100
Εννενήντα	Εκατό
`ĕ`N-N`ĕ`-N`ĒĒ`N-D`ah`	`ĕ`-K`ah`-T`O`

1,000	1,000,000
Χίλια	Ένα εκατομμύριο
H`ĕ`-LY`ah`	`ĕ`-N`ah`
	`ĕ`-K`ah`-T`O`-M`ĒĒ`-R`ĒĒ`-O

DICTIONARY

Each English entry is followed
by the Greek word in the
Greek alphabet followed by
the EPLS Vowel Symbol System.

If a word is masculine, feminine or neuter it will
be indicated by an (m) for masculine and (f) for
feminine and (n) for neuter as shown below.

GREEK PUNCTUATION

Period is indicated (.) as in English.

Comma is indicated (,) as in English.

Question mark is indicated (;). It looks like an
English semicolon.

A Greek semicolon looks like this (·).

Below is an example of the English (?) and
corresponding Greek question mark (;).

Why?

Γιατί;

Y@h-T€€

A

a lot πολύ Pⓞ-LⒺⓈ

able ικανός ⒺⓀⓐⓗⲚⓄⓈ

accident ατύχημα ⓐⓗ-TⒺⒽⒺ-Mⓐⓗ

accommodation κατάλυμα Kⓐⓗ-Tⓐⓗ-LⒺ-Mⓐⓗ

account λογαριασμός LⓄ-Gⓐⓗ-RⒺ-ⓐⓗⓈ-MⓄⓈ

address διεύθυνση THⒺ-ⓔF-THⒺN-SⒺ

admission ticket είσοδος ⒺⲤ-SⓄ-THⓄⓈ

afraid (to be) φοβάμαι FⓄ-VⓐⓗⲘⒺ

after μετά MⒺ-Tⓐⓗ

afternoon απόγευμα ⓐⓗ-PⓄ-YⒺV-Mⓐⓗ

agency πρακτορείο PRⓐⓗK-TⓄ-RⒺ-Ⓞ

air-conditioning κλιματισμός
KLⒺ-Mⓐⓗ-TⒺⓈ-MⓄⓈ

aircraft αεροσκάφος ⓐⓗ-Ⓔ-RⓄ-SKⓐⓗⲪⓄⓈ

airline αεροπορική εταιρία
ⓐⓗ-Ⓔ-RⓄ-PⓄ-RⒺ-KⒺ Ⓔ-TⒺ-RⒺ-ⓐⓗ

airport αεροδρόμιο ⓐⓗ-Ⓔ-RⓄ-THRⓄ-MⒺ-Ⓞ

aisle διάδρομος THⒺ-ⓐⓗ-THRⓄ-MⓄⓈ

all όλες Ⓞ-LⒺⓈ

almost σχεδόν HⒺ-THⓄN

alone μόνος (m) / μόνη (f) MⓄ-NⓄⓈ / MⓄ-NⒺ (n)

also επίσης ⓔ-PⒺ-SⒺⓈ

always πάντα PⓐN-Dⓐʰ

ambulance ασθενοφόρο ⓐʰS-THⓔ-NⓄ-FⓄ-RⓄ

American Αμερικάνος (m) / Αμερικάνα (f)
ⓐʰ-Mⓔ-Rⓔ-Kⓐʰ-NⓄS / ⓐʰ-Mⓔ-Rⓔ-Kⓐʰ-Nⓐʰ

and και Kⓔ

another άλλος (m) / άλλη (f) / άλλο (n)
ⓐʰ-LⓄS / ⓐʰ-LⓔE / ⓐʰ-LⓄ

apartment διαμέρισμα THⓔE-ⓐʰ-Mⓔ-RⓔES-Mⓐʰ

appetizers ορεκτικά Ⓞ-RⓔK-TⓔE-Kⓐʰ

apple μήλο MⓔE-LⓄ

appointment ραντεβού BⓐʰN-Dⓔ-Vⓞⓞ

April Απρίλιος ⓐʰ-PRⓔE-LⓔE-ⓄS

arrivals άφιξη ⓐʰ-FⓔEK-SⓔES

ashtray τασάκι Tⓐʰ-Sⓐʰ-KⓔE

aspirin ασπιρίνη ⓐʰS-PⓔE-RⓔE-NⓔE

attention προσοχή PRⓄ-SⓄ-HⓔE

August Αύγουστος ⓐʰF-Gⓞⓞ̲S-TⓄS

Australia Αυστραλία ⓐʰF-STRⓐʰ-LⓔE-ⓐʰ

Australian Αυστραλός (m) / Αυστραλέζα (f)
ⓐʰF-STRⓐʰ-LⓄS / ⓐʰF-STRⓐʰ-Lⓔ-Zⓐʰ

author συγγραφέας SⓔEN-GRⓐʰ-Fⓔ-ⓐʰS

automobile αυτοκίνητο ⓐʰF-TⓄ-KⓔE-NⓔE-TⓄ

autumn φθινόπωρο FTHⓔE-NⓄ-PⓄ-RⓄ

avenue λεωφόρος LĒ-O-FŌ-BOS

awful τρομερός ah-PĒ-SĒE-OS

B

baby μωρό MO-BŌ

bacon μπέϊκον BĒ-ĒE-KON

bad κακός Kah-KOS

bag τσάντα TSah-Dah

baggage αποσκευές ah-PO-SKĒ-VĒS

bakery φούρνος FOOB-NOS

banana μπανάνα Bah-Nah-Nah

Band-Aid επίδεσμος Hah'N-ZO-PLah'ST

bank τράπεζα TBah-PĒ-Zah

barbershop κουρείο KOO-BĒ-ahS

bartender μπάρμαν Bah'B-Mah'N

bath μπάνιο Bah'N-YO

bathing suit μαγιώ Mah-YO

bathroom μπάνιο LOO-THBŌ

battery μπαταρία Bah-Tah-BĒE-ah

beach παραλία Pah-Bah-LĒE-ah

beautiful όμορφος (m) / όμορφη (f) / όμορφο (n)
O-MOB-FOS / O-MOB-FĒE / O-MOB-FO

beauty shop μαγαζί με καλλυντικά
Mah-Gah-ZEE MEe Kah-LEEN-DEE-Kah

bed κρεβάτι KREe-Vah-TEE

beef βοδινό κρέας VO-THEE-NO KREe-ahS

beer μπύρα BEE-Rah

bellman βοηθός ξενοδοχείου
VO-Ee-THO'S KSEe-NO-THO-HEe-oo

belt ζώνη ZO'-NEE

big μεγάλος (m) / μεγάλη (f) / μεγάλο (n)
MEe-Gah-LOS / MEe-Gah-LEe / MEe-Gah-LO

bill λογαριασμός LO-Gah-B-Yah-S-MO'S

black μαύρο Mah-VROS

blanket κουβέρτα Koo-VEe-R-Tah

blue μπλε BLEe

boat βάρκα Vah-B-Kah

book βιβλίο VEE-VLEe-O

bookstore βιβλιοπωλείο VEE-VLEe-O PO-LEe-O

border (country) σύνορα SEE-NO-Rah

boy αγόρι ah-GO-REe

bracelet βραχιόλι VRah-HEe-O-LEe

brakes φρένο FREe-NO

bread ψωμί PSO-MEeN

breakfast πρωινό PRO-EE-NO'

brother αδελφός ⓐ-THⓔL-FⓄS

brown καφέ Kⓐ-Fⓔ

brush βούρτσα VⓄⓄB-TSⓐ

building κτίριο KTⓔⓔ-Bⓔⓔ-Ⓞ

bus λεωφορείο Lⓔ-Ⓞ-FⓄ-Bⓔⓔ-Ⓞ

bus station σταθμός λεωφορείων
STⓐTH-MⓄS Lⓔ-Ⓞ-FⓄ-Bⓔⓔ-ⓄⓄN

bus stop στάση λεωφορείου
STⓐ-Sⓔⓔ Lⓔ-Ⓞ-FⓄ-Bⓔⓔ-ⓄⓄ

business επιχείρηση ⓔ-Pⓔⓔ-Hⓔⓔ-Bⓔⓔ-Sⓔⓔ

butter βούτυρο VⓄⓄ-Tⓔⓔ-BⓄ

buy (I) αγοράζω ⓐ-GⓄ-Bⓐ-ZⓄ

C

cab ταξί TⓐK-Sⓔⓔ

call (to) καλώ Kⓐ-LⓄ

camera κάμερα Kⓐ-Mⓔ-Bⓐ

Canada Καναδάς Kⓐ-Nⓐ-THⓐS

Canadian Καναδός (m) / Καναδή (m)
Kⓐ-Nⓐ-THⓄS / Kⓐ-Nⓐ-THⓔⓔ

candy καραμέλα Kⓐ-Bⓐ-Mⓔ-Lⓐ

car αμάξι ⓐF-TⓄ-Kⓔ-Nⓔⓔ-TⓄ

carrot καρότο Kⓐ-BⓄ-TⓄ

castle κάστρο Kⓐ-STBⓄ

celebration γιορτή YOB-T℮

center κέντρο K℮N-TBO

cereal (cold) κορν φλεϊκς KOBN FL@KS

chair καρέκλα K@h-B℮-KL@h

champagne σαμπάνια S@M-P@hN-Y@h

change (to) αλλαγή @h-L@h-Y℮

change (money) ψιλά S℮-L@h

cheap φτηνός (m) / φτηνη (f) / φτηνό (n)
  FT℮-NO′S / FT℮-N℮ / FT℮-NO′

check (restaurant bill) λογαριασμός
  LO-G@B-Y@hS-MO′S

cheers! γειά μας Y@h-M@hS

cheese τυρί T℮-B℮

chicken κοτόπουλο KO-TO′-Poo-LO

child παιδί P℮-TH℮

chocolate σοκολάτα SO-KO-L@h-T@h

church εκκλησία ℮K-L℮-S℮-@h

cigar πούρο Poo-BO

cigarette τσιγάρο TS℮-G@h-BO

city πόλη PO′-L℮

clean καθαρό K@h-TH@h-BO′

close (to) κλείνω KL℮-NO

closed κλειστός (m) / κλειστή (f) / κλειστό (n)
KLEE-STOS / KLEE-STEE / KLEE-STO

clothes ρούχα ROO-Hah

cocktail κοκτέϊλ KOK-TAY-EEL

coffee καφές Kah-FES

cold (temperature) κρύο KREE-OS

comb χτένα HTEN-ah

computer υπολογιστής EE-PO-LO-YEE-STEES

concert συναυλία SEEN-ahVL-EE-ah

conference σύσκεψη SEE-SKEE-PSEE

congratulations συγχαρητήρια
SEE-Hah-REE-TEE-REE-ah

copy machine φωτοτυπικό μηχάνιμα
FO-TO-TEE-PEE-KO MEE-Hah-NEE-Mah

corn καλαμπόκι Kah-Lah-BO-KEE

cough syrup συρόπι για το βήχα
SEE-RO-PEE Yah TON VEE-Hah

crab καβούρι Kah-VOO-REE

cream κρέμα KREE-Mah

credit card πιστωτική κάρτα
PEE-STO-TEE-KEE KahR-Tah

cup φλιτζάνι FLEET-Zah-NEE

customs τελωνείο TEE-LO-NEE-O

D

dance (I) χορεύω HO-Rĕ́-GO

dangerous επικίνδυνος ĕ-Pĕĕ-KĕĕN-THĕĕ-NOS

date (day) ημερομηνία ĕĕ-Mĕ̌-RO-Mĕĕ-Nĕ́-ah

day ημέρα Mĕ́-Rah

December Δεκέμβριος THĕ́-Kĕ̈M-VRĕĕ-OS

delicious νόστιμος NO-STĕĕ-MOS

dentist οδοντίατρος O-THON-Dĕ́-ah-TROS

deodorant αποσμητικό ah-POS-Mĕĕ-Tĕĕ-KO

department τμήμα TMĕĕ-Mah

departure αναχώρηση ah-Nah-HO-Rĕĕ-Sĕĕ

dessert επιδόρπιο ĕ-Pĕĕ-THOR-Pĕĕ-O

diabetic διαβητικός THĕĕ-ah-Vĕĕ-Tĕĕ-KOS

diarrhea διάρροια THĕĕ-ah-R-Rĕĕ-ah

dictionary λεξικό Lĕ̈-KSĕĕ-KO

dining room τραπεζαρία TRah-Pĕ̌-Zah-Rĕ́-ah

dinner βραδινό VRah-THĕĕ-NO

direction κατεύθυνση Kah-Tĕ̈F-THĕĕN-Sĕĕ

dirty βρώμικος VRO-Mĕĕ-KO

disabled ανάπηρος ah-Nah-Pĕĕ-ROS

discount έκπτωση ĕ̈K-PTO-Sĕĕ

distance απόσταση ah-PO-STah-Sĕĕ

dizziness ζαλή Zah-LEE

doctor ιατρός Yah-TROS

dollar δολάριο MO-Lah-REE-O

down κάτω Kah-TO

downtown κέντρο KEN-DRO

drink (beverage) ποτό PEE-NO

drugstore φαρμακείο FahR-Mah-KEE-ah

dry cleaner καθαριστήριο Kah-Tah-REES-TEE-REE-O

duck σκύβω Pah-PEE-ah

E

ear αυτί ahF-TEE

ear drops σταγωνες για τα αυτιά
STah-GO-NES Yah Tah ahF-TEE-ah

early νωρίς NO-REES

east Ανατολή ah-Nah-TO-LEE-Kah

easy εύκολο EF-KO-LO

eat (to) τρώω TRO-O

egg αυγό ahV-GO

electricity ηλεκτρικό EE-LEK-TREE-KO

elevator ασανσέρ ah-SahN-SER

e-mail (E-mail as in English)

embassy πρεσβεία PREE-SVEE-ah

emergency έκτακτη ανάγκη
ⓔK-TⓐK-TⒺ ⓐh-Nⓐh-KⒺ

England Αγγλία ⓐN-G̲LⒺ-ⓐh

English Αγγλικά ⓐN-G̲LⒺ-Kⓐh

enough! αρκετά ⓐhB̲-Kⓔ-Tⓐh

entrance είσοδος Ⓔ-SⓄ-T̲H̲Ⓞs

envelope φάκελος Fⓐh-Kⓔ-LⓄs

evening βράδυ VBⓐh-T̲H̲Ⓔ

everything όλα ⓄL-ⓐh

excellent υπέροχα Ⓔ-Pⓔ-BⓄ-H̲ⓐh

excuse me συγνώμη SⒺ-G̲NⓄ-MⒺ

exit έξοδος ⓔK-SⓄ-T̲H̲Ⓞs

expensive ακριβό ⓐh-KBⒺ-VⓄ

eye μάτι Mⓐh-TⒺ

eye drops κολλύριο KⓄ-LⒺ-BⒺ-Ⓞ

F

face πρόσωπο PBⓄ-SⓄ-PⓄ

far μακριά Mⓐh-KBⒺ-ⓐh

fare εισητήριο Ⓔ-SⒺ-TⒺ-BⒺ-Ⓞ

fast γρήγορα GBⒺ-G̲Ⓞ-Bⓐh

father πατέρας Pⓐh-Tⓔ̈B-ⓐhS

fax, fax machine φαξ Fⓐh KS

February Φεβρουάριος FⒺV-Bⓞⓞ-ⓐⓗ-BⒺⒺ-Oⓢ

fee αμοιβή ⓐⓗ-MⒺⒺ-VⒺ

few λίγοι LⒺⒺ-Gⓞ

film (movie) σινεμά SⒺⒺN-Ⓔ-Mⓐⓗ

film (camera) φιλμ FⒺLM

finger δάκτυλο THⓐⓗK-TⒺⒺ-Lⓞ

fire (heat) φωτιά Fⓞ-TⒺⒺ-ⓐⓗ

fire! (emergency) φωτιά Fⓞ-TⒺⒺ-ⓐⓗ

fire extinguisher πυροσβεστήρας
PⒺⒺ-Bⓞⓢ-VⒺⓢ-TⒺⒺB-ⓐⓗⓢ

first πρώτος PBⓞ-Tⓞⓢ

fish ψάρι PSⓐⓗ-BⒺⒺ

flight πτήση PTⒺⒺ-SⒺⒺ

florist shop ανθοπωλείο ⓐⓗN-THⓞ-Pⓞ-LⒺⒺ-ⓞ

flower λουλούδι Lⓞⓞ-Lⓞⓞ-THⒺⒺ

food φαγητό Fⓐⓗ-YⒺⒺ-Tⓞ

foot πόδι Pⓞ-THⒺⒺ

fork πηρούνι PⒺⒺ-Bⓞⓞ-NⒺⒺ

french fries πατάτες τηγανιτές
Pⓐⓗ-Tⓐⓗ-TⒺⓢ TⒺⒺ-Gⓐⓗ-NⒺⒺ-TⒺⓢ

fresh φρέσκος FBⒺⓢ-Kⓞⓢ

Friday παρασκευή Pⓐⓗ-Bⓐⓗ-SKⒺ-VⒺⒺ

fried τηγανηιτός TⒺⒺ-Gⓐⓗ-NⒺⒺ-Tⓞⓢ

friend φίλος F(EE)'-L(O)S

fruit φρούτο FR(OO)'-T(O)

funny αστείο (AH)S-T(EE)-(O)'S

G

gas station βενζινάδικο V(Ĕ)N-Z(EE)-N(AH)'-TH(EE)-K(O)

gasoline βενζίνη V(Ĕ)N-Z(EE)'-N(EE)

gate θύρα TH(EE)'-R(AH)

gift δώρο TH(O)'-R(O)

girl κορίτσι K(O)-R(EE)'T-S(EE)

glass (drinking) ποτήρι P(O)-T(EE)'-R(EE)

glasses (eye) γυαλιά Y(AH)-L(EE)-(AH)'

gloves γάντια G(AH)'N-D(EE)-(AH)

go (to) πήγαινε P(EE)-Y(Ĕ)-N(Ĕ)'

gold χρυσό H̤R(EE)-S(O)'

golf γκολφ G(O)LF

golf course γήπεδο γκολφ Y(EE)'-P(Ĕ)-TH(O) G(O)LF

good καλό K(AH)-L(O)'

good-bye γειά σας Y(AH)'-S(AH)S

grape σταφύλι ST(AH)-F(EE)'-L(EE)

grateful ευγνώμων (Ĕ)V-GN(O)'-M(O)N

gray γκρι GR(EE)

green πράσινο PR(AH)'-S(EE)-N(O)

grocery store μανάβικο Mah-Nah-VEE-KO

group γκρουπ GRooP

guide ξεναγός KSEN-ah-GOS

H

hair μαλλιά Mah-LEE-ah

hairbrush βούρτσα VooR-TSah

haircut κούρεμα Koo-REE-Mah

ham ζαμπόν Zah-BON

hamburger χάμπεργκερ Hah M-BER-GER

hand χέρι HEE-REE

happy ευτυχισμένος EF-TEE-HEES-MEE-NOS

have (to) έχω E-HO

he αυτός ah F-TOS

head κεφάλι KE-Fah-LEE

headache πονοκέφαλος PO-NO-KE-Fah-LOS

health club (gym) γυμναστήριο
YEEM-Nah-STEE-REE-O

heart καρδιά Kah R-THEE-ah

heart condition έχω καρδιά
E-HO Kah R-THEE-ah

heat (weather) ζέστη ZE-STEE

heat (in-door heating) θέρμανση THER-Mah N-SEE

hello γειά σας Y@h-S@hS

help! (emergency) βοήθεια V@@-@-TH@-@h

holiday διακοπές TH@-@h-K@-P@S

hospital νοσοκομείο N@-S@-K@-M@-@

hotel ξενοδοχείο KS@N-@-TH@-H@-@

hour ώρα @-R@h

how πώς P@S

hurry up! βιάσου V@-@h-S@@

husband σύζυγος S@-Z@-G@S

I

I εγώ @-H@

ice πάγος P@h-G@S

ice cream παγωτό P@h-G@-T@

ice cubes παγάκια P@h-G@h-K@-@h

important σημαντικός S@-M@h-D@-K@S

indigestion δισπεψεία TH@S-P@-PS@-@h

information πληροφορίες PL@-R@-F@-R@-@S

internet Ιντερνετ Καφέ (Internet Café as in English)

interpreter διερμηνέας TH@-@R-M@-NG@-@hS

island νηαί N@-S@

J

jacket σακάκι S@h-K@h-K@

jam μαρμελάδα Mah-B-M̃ĕ-L-ah-TH-ah

January Ιανουάριος ĔE-ah-N-oo-ah-REE-OS

jewelry κοσμήματα K-O-S-M-ĒE-M-ah-Tah

jewelry store κοσμηματοπωλείο
K-O-S-M-ĒE-M-ah-T-O-P-O-L-ĒE-O

job δουλειά TH-oo-L-EE-ah

juice χυμός H̃-ĒE-M-OS

July Ιούλιος ĔE-oo-L-ĒE-OS

June Ιούνιος ĔE-oo-N-ĒE-OS

K

ketchup κέτσαπ K-ĕ-T-S-ah-P

key κλειδί KL-ĒE-TH-ĒE

kiss φιλί F-ĒE-L-O

knife μαχαίρι M-ah-H̃-ĒE-B-EE

know (I) ξέρω KS-ĕ-B-O

L

ladies (toilet) γυναικών Y-ĒE-N-ĕ-K-ON

lady κυρία K-ĒE-B-EE-ah

lamb αρνί ah-B-N-ĒE

language γλώσσα GL-O-S-ah

large μεγάλος M-ĕ-G-ah-L-OS

late αργά ah-B-G-ah

laundry πληντύριο PL㊉-D㊉-B㊉-O

lawyer δικηγόρος TH㊉-K㊉-G㊉-R㊉S

left (direction) αριστερά ah-B㊉-ST㊉-Bah

leg πόδι P㊉-TH㊉

lemon λεμόνι L㊉-M㊉-N㊉

less λιγότερο L㊉-G㊉-T㊉-B㊉

letter γράμμα GBah-Mah

lettuce μαρούλι Mah-B㊀-L㊉

light φως F㊉S

like (I) μου αρέσει M㊀-ah-B㊉-S㊉

lips χείλια H㊉-L㊉-ah

lipstick κραγιόν KBah-Y㊉N

little (amount) λίγο L㊉-G㊉

little (size) μικρό M㊉-KB㊉

live (to) μένω M㊉-N㊉

lobster αστακός ahS-Tah-K㊉S

long μακρύ Mah-KB㊉

lost έχω χαθεί ㊉-H㊉ Hah-TH㊉

love αγάπη ah-G㊍-P㊉

luck τύχη T㊉-H㊉

luggage αποσκευές ah-P㊉S-K㊉-V㊉S

lunch μεσημεριανό M㊉-S㊉-M㊉-B㊉-ah-N㊉

M

maid καμαριέρα K@h-M@h-B⒠-⒠-B@h

makeup μακιγιάζ M@h-K⒠-Y@hZ

man άνδρας @hN-THB@hS

map χάρτης H@hB-T⒠SK

March Μάρτιος M@hB-T⒠-⒪S

market αγορά @h-G⒪-B@h

match (light) σπίρτο SP⒠B-T@h

May Μάιος M@h-⒠-⒪S

mayonnaise μαγιονέζα M@h-Y⒪-N⒠-Z@h

meal γεύμα Y⒠V-M@h

meat κρέας KB⒠-@hS

mechanic μηχανικός M⒠-H@h-N⒠-K⒪S

meeting σύσκεψη S⒠-SK⒠-PS⒠

mens' restroom τουαλέτα ανδρών
T⒪⒪-@h-L⒠-T@h @hN-THB⒪N

menu μενού M⒠-N⒪⒪

message μήνυμα M⒠-N⒠-M@h

milk γάλα G@h-L@h

mineral water μεταλικό νερό
M⒠-T@h-L⒠-K⒪ N⒠-B⒪

minute λεπτό L⒠P-T⒪

Miss Δεσποινὶς TH⒠S-P⒠-N⒠S

mistake λάθος L@-THⓄS

misunderstanding παρεξήγηση
P@-Rⓔ-KSⒺ-Gⓔ-SⒺ

moment στιγμή STⒺ-GMⓔ-Gⓔ́

Monday Δευτέρα THⓄF-Tⓔ-R@

money λεφτά Lⓔ́F-T@

month μήνας MⒺ́-N@S

monument μνημείο MNⒺ-Mⓔ́-Ⓞ

more περισσότερο Pⓔ-Rⓔ-SⓄ́-Tⓔ-RⓄ

morning πρωί PRⓄ-Ⓔ

mother μητέρα MⒺ-Tⓔ-R@

mountain βουνό Vⓞⓞ-NⓄ́

movies σινεμά SⒺN-ⓔ-M@

Mr. κύριος KⒺ-Rⓔ-ⓄS

Mrs. κυρία KⒺ-Rⓔ-@

much πολύ PⓄ-Lⓔ

museum μουσείο Mⓞⓞ-SⒺ-Ⓞ

mushrooms μανιτάρια M@-NⒺ-T@-RⒺ

music μουσική Mⓞⓞ-SⒺ-Kⓔ

mustard μουστάρδα Mⓞⓞ-ST@B-TH@

N

name όνομα, Ⓞ́-NⓄ-M@

napkin πετσέτα Pⓔ-TSⓔ-T@

near κοντά KON-Dah

neck σβέρκος SVER-KOS

need (I) χρειάζομαι HREE-ah-ZO-MÊ

never ποτέ PO-TÊ

news stand περίπτερο PÊ-REEP-TÊ-RO

newspaper εφημερίδα Ê-FEE-MÊ-REE-THah

night νύχτα NEEH-Tah

nightclub κλαμπ KLahB

no όχι OK-HEE

no smoking (forbidden) απαγορεύεται το κάπνισμα
ah-Pah-GO-RÊ-VÊ-TÊ TO KahP-NEES-Mah

noon μεσημέρι MÊ-SEE-MÊ-REE

north Βορράς VO-REE-ah

November Νοέμβριος NO-ÊM-VREE—OS

now τώρα TO-Rah

number νούμερο NOO-MÊ-RO

nurse νοσόκομα NO-SO-KO-Mah

O

occupied κατειλημμένο Kah-TEE-LEE-MÊ-NO

ocean ωκεανός O-KÊ-ah-NOS

October Οκτώβριος OK-TO-VREE-OS

oil λάδι Lah-THEE

omelet ομελέτα Ⓞ-Mⓔ-Lⓔ́-Tⓐ

one-way (traffic) μονόδρομος MⓄ-NⓄ́-THRⓄ-MⓄS

onion κρεμμύδι KRⓔ-Mⓔ-THⓔ

on-line (on-line as in English)

open ανοικτό ⓐ-NⓔK-TⓄ́

opera όπερα Ⓞ́-Pⓔ-Bⓐ

operator χειριστής Hⓔ-Bⓔ-STⓔ́S

orange (color) πορτοκαλί PⓄB-TⓄ-Kⓐ-Lⓔ́

order (to) να παραγγείλω Nⓐ Pⓐ-Bⓐ-Gⓔ́-LⓄ

original αυθεντικός ⓐB-THⓔ-Tⓔ-KⓄ́S

owner κάτοχος Kⓐ-TⓄK-HⓄS

oysters στρείδια STBⓔ-THⓔ-ⓐ

P

package πακέτο Pⓐ-Kⓔ́-TⓄ

pain πόνος PⓄ́-NⓄS

painting πίνακας Pⓔ-Nⓐ-Kⓐs

paper χαρτί HⓐB-Tⓔ

parking πάρκινγκ Pⓐ́B-KⓔNG

partner (business) συνέταιρος Sⓔ-Nⓔ́-Tⓔ-BⓄS

party πάρτυ Pⓐ́B-Tⓔ

passenger επιβάτης ⓔ-Pⓔ-Vⓐ-Tⓔ́S

passport διαβατήριο THⓔ-ⓐ-Vⓐ-Tⓔ́-Bⓔ-Ⓞ

pasta μακαρόνια Mah-Kah-RON-Yah

pastry γλυκά GLEE-Kah

pen στιλό STEE-LO

pencil μολύβι MO-LEE-VEE

pepper πιπεριά PEE-Pē-REE-ah

perfume άρωμα ah-RO-Mah

person άτομο ah-TO-MO

pharmacist φαρμακοποιός FahR-Mah-KO-PEE-OS

pharmacy φαρμακείο FahR-Mah-KEE-O

phone book τελεφωνικός κατάλογος
TEE-Lē-FO-NEE-KOS Kah-Tah-LO-GahS

photo φωτογραφία FO-TO-GRah-FEE-ah

photographer φωτογράφος FO-TO-GRah-FOS

pillow μαξιλάρι MahK-SEE-Lah-REE

pink ροζ ROZ

pizza πίτσα PEET-Sah

plastic πλαστικός PLahS-TEE-KOS

plate πιάτο PEE-ah-TO

please παρακαλώ Pah-Rah-Kah-LO

pleasure ευχαρίστηση ēF-Hah-REE-STEE-SEE

police αστυνομία ahS-TEE-NO-MEE-ah

police station τμήμα TMEE-Mah

pork χοιρινό HEE-REE-NO

porter βοηθός VO-EE-THOS

post office ταχυδρομείο Tah-HEE-THRO-MEE-O

postcard καρτ-ποστάλ KahRT POS-TahL

potatoes πατάτες Pah-Tah-TēS

pregnant (I'm) είμαι έγκυος EE-MEE ēN-KEE-OS

prescription συνταγή γιατρού
SEEN-Dah-YEE Yah-TRO

price τιμή TEE-MEE

problem πρόβλημα PRO-VLEE-Mah

public δημόσιος THEE-MO-SEE-O

public telephone καρτοτηλέφωνο
KahR-TO-TEE-Lē-FO-NO

pure αγνό ahG-NO

purple μωβ MOV

purse πορτοφόλι POR-TO-FO-LEE

Q

quality ποιότητα PEE-O-TEE-Tah

question ερώτηση ē-RO-TEE-SEE

quickly γρήγορα GREE-GO-Rah

quiet! (be) ησυχία EE-SEE-HEE-ah

quit (to) παραιτούμαι Pah-Rē-TOO-Mē

R

radio ράδιο R@-TH㏕-O

railroad σιδηρόδρομος
S㏕-TH㏕-RO'-THRO-M㏕-K@S

rain βροχή VR@-H㏕

raincoat αδιάβροχο @-TH㏕-@-VRO-HO

ramp ράμπα R@M-P@

razor blades ξυράφι KS㏕-R@-F㏕

ready έτοιμο @-T㏕-MOS

receipt απόδειξη @-PO'-TH㏕K-S㏕

recommend (I) συνιστώ S㏕-N㏕-STO'

red κόκκινο KO'-K㏕-N@S

repeat! επαναλάβετε @-P@-N@-L@M-V@-T@

reservation κράτηση KR@-T㏕-S㏕

restaurant εστιατόριο @S-T㏕-@-TO'-R㏕-O

return (to) επιστρέφω @-P㏕S-TR@-FO

rice (cooked) ρύζι R㏕-S㏕

rich πλούσιος PL∞-S㏕-@S

right (correct) σωστό SO-STO'

right (direction) δεξιά TH@K-S㏕-@

road δρόμος THRO'-MOS

room δωμάτιο THO-M@-T㏕-O

round-trip με επιστροφή M@ @-P㏕S-TRO-F㏕

S

safe (hotel) ασφαλές ⓐS-Fⓐ-Lⓔ́S

salad σαλάτα Sⓐ-Lⓐ-Tⓐ

sale πώληση Pⓞ́-Lⓔ-Sⓔ

salmon σολομός Sⓞ-Lⓞ-Mⓞ́S

salt αλάτι ⓐ-Lⓐ́-Tⓔ

sandwich σάντουιτς SⓐND-WⓔTS

Saturday Σάββατο Sⓐ́-Vⓐ-Tⓞ

scissors ψαλίδι PSⓐ-Lⓔ́-Tⓔ

sculpture γλυπτό GLⓔP-Tⓞ́

seafood θαλασσινά THⓐ-Lⓐ-Sⓔ-Nⓐ́

season εποχή ⓔ-Pⓞ-Hⓔ́

seat θέση THⓔ́-Sⓔ

secretary γραμματέας GRⓐ-Mⓐ-Tⓔ́-ⓐ

section κομμάτι Kⓞ-Mⓐ́-Tⓔ

section τομέας Tⓞ-Mⓔ́-ⓐS

September Σεπτέμβριος SⓔP-Tⓔ́M-VRⓔ-ⓞS

service σέρβις Sⓔ́B-VⓔS

several μερικά Mⓔ-Rⓔ-Kⓐ́

shampoo σαμπουάν SⓐM-Pⓞⓞ-ⓐ́N

sheets (bed) σεντόνια SⓔN-Dⓞ́-Nⓔ-ⓐ

shirt πουκάμισο Pⓞⓞ-Kⓐ́-Mⓔ-Sⓞ

shoe store κατάστημα υποδημάτων
Kah-Tah-STEE-Mah EE-PO-THEE-Mah-TON

shoes παπούτσια Pah-POOT-SEE-ah

shopping center εμπορικό κέντρο
E-BO-REE-KO KEN-DRO

shower μπάνιο BahN-YO

shrimp γαρίδες Gah-REE-THES

sick άρρωστος ah-ROS-TOS

sign (display) πινακίδα PEE-Nah-KEE-THah

signature υπογραφή EE-PO-GRah-FEE

single μονό MO-NO

sister αδελφή ah-THEL-FEE

size μέγεθος ME-YE-THOS

skin δέρμα THER-Mah

skirt φούστα FOO-STah

sleeve μανίκι Mah-NEE-KEE

slowly σιγά SEE-Gah

small μικρό MEE-KRO

smile (I) χαμόγελο Hah-MO-YE-LO

smoke (I) καπνίζω KahP-NEE-ZO

soap σαπούνι Sah-POO-NEE

socks κάλτσες KahLT-SES

some μερικά ME-REE-Kah

something κάτι K@h-T@

sometimes μερικές φορές
M@-R@-K@S F@-B@S

soon σύντομα S@N-D@-M@h

sorry (I am) συγγνώμη S@G-N@-M@

soup σούπα S@-P@h

south Νότος N@-T@S

souvenir σουβενίρ S@-V@-N@R

Spanish (language) Ισπανικά @-SP@h-N@-K@h

Spanish (person) Ισπανός (m) / Ισπανίδα (f)
@-SP@h-N@S / @-SP@h-N@-D@h

speed ταχύτητα T@h-H@-T@-T@h

spoon κουτάλι K@-T@h-L@

sport σπορ SP@R

spring (season) Άνοιξη @h-N@K-S@

stairs σκάλες SK@h-L@S

stamp γραμματόσημο GB@h-M@h-T@-S@-M@

station σταθμός ST@hT-M@S

steak μπριζόλα BB@-Z@-L@h

stomach στομάχι ST@-M@h-H@

stop! σταμάτα ST@h-M@h-T@h

store κατάστημα K@h-T@h-ST@-M@h

storm καταιγίδα K@h-T@-Y@-TH@h

straight ahead ευθεία ⒠F-TH㋎-ⓐ

strawberry φράουλα FⓇⓐ-㋧-Lⓐ

street δρόμος THⓇⓄ-MⓄS

string κορδόνι KⓄⒷ-THⓄ-N㋎

subway υπόγειος M㋎-TⓇⓄ

sugar ζάχαρη Zⓐ-Hⓐ-Ⓡ㋎

suit (clothes) κοστούμι K㋧S-T㋧-M㋎

suitcase βαλίτσα Vⓐ-L㋎T-Sⓐ

summer καλοκαίρι Kⓐ-LⓄ-K㋎-Ⓡ㋎

sun ήλιος ㋎-L㋎-ⓄS

Sunday Κυριακή K㋎-Ⓡ㋎-ⓐ-K㋎

sunglasses γυαλιά ήλιου Yⓐ-L㋎-ⓐ ㋎-L㋎-㋧

suntan lotion αντιλιακό ⓐ-D㋎-L㋎-ⓐ-KⓄ

supermarket σούπερ μάρκετ
    S㋧-PⒺⓇ MⓐⒷ-KⒺT

surprise έκπληξη ⒠K-PLⒺK-S㋎

sweet γλυκό GLⒺ-KⓄ

swim (I) κολυμπώ KⓄ-L㋎-ⒷⓄ

swimming pool πισίνα P㋎-S㋎-Nⓐ

Synagogue Συναγωγή S㋎-Nⓐ-GⓄ-Y㋎

T

table τραπέζι TⓇⓐ-P㋎-Z㋎

tampon ταμπόν TⓐⓜM-BⓄN

tape (sticky) σελοτέηπ SⒺ-LⓄ-TⒺ-ⒺP

tape recorder κασετόφωνο Kⓐh-SⒺ-TⓄ-FⓄ-NⓄ

tax φόρος FⓄ-RⓄS

taxi ταξί TⓐhK-SⒺ

tea τσάι TSⓐh-Ⓔ

telephone τηλέφωνο TⒺ-LⒺ-FⓄ-NⓄ

television τηλεόραση TⒺ-LⒺ-Ⓞ-Rⓐh-SⒺ

temperature (room/weather) θερμοκρασία
  THⒺR-MⓄ-KRⓐh-SⒺ-ⓐh

temperature (fever) πυρετός PⒺ-RⒺ-TⓄS

tennis τένις TⒺ-NⒺS

tennis court γήπεδο του τέννις
  YⒺ-PⒺ-THⓄ Tⓞⓞ TⒺ-NⒺS

thank you! ευχαριστώ ⒺF-HⓐhR-ⒺS-TⓄ

that εκείνο Ⓔ-KⒺ-NⓄ

theater (movie) θέατρο THⒺ-ⓐh-TRⓄ

there εκεί Ⓔ-KⒺ

they αυτοί (m) / αυτές (f) / αυτά (n)
  ⓐhF-TⒺ / ⓐhF-TⒺS / ⓐhF-Tⓐh

this αυτό ⓐhF-TⓄ

thread κλωστή KLⓄ-STⒺ

throat λαιμός LⒺ-MⓄS

Thursday Πέμπτη PⒺMP-TⒺⒺ

ticket εισιτήριο ⒺⒺ-SⒺⒺ-TⒺⒺ-RⒺⒺ-Ⓞ

tie γραβάτα G̲Rⓐⓗ-Vⓐⓗ-Tⓐⓗ

time ώρα Ⓞ-Rⓐⓗ

tip (gratuity) φιλοδώρημα FⒺⒺ-LⓄ-THⓄ-RⒺⒺ-Mⓐⓗ

tire λάστιχο LⓐⓗS-TⒺⒺ-HⓄ

toast (bread) τοστ TⓄST

tobacco καπνός KⓐⓗP-NⓄS

today σήμερα SⒺⒺ-MⒺ-Rⓐⓗ

toe δάκτυλο TH̲ⓐⓗK-TⒺⒺ-LⓄ

together μαζί Mⓐⓗ-ZⒺⒺ

toilet τουαλέτα TⓄⓄ-ⓐⓗ-LⒺ-Tⓐⓗ

toilet paper χαρτί υγείας HⓐⓗR-TⒺⒺ ⒺⒺ-YⒺⒺ-ⓐⓗS

tomato τομάτα DⓄ-Mⓐⓗ-TⒺS

tomorrow αύριο ⓐⓗV-RⒺⒺ-Ⓞ

tooth δόντι TH̲ⓄN-DⒺⒺ

toothache πονόδοντος PⓄ-NⓄ-TH̲ⓄN-DⓄS

toothbrush οδοντόβουρτσα
ⓄO-TH̲ⓄN-DⓄ-VⓄB-STⓐⓗ

toothpaste οδοντόκρεμα Ⓞ-TH̲ⓄN-DⓄ-KRⒺ-Mⓐⓗ

toothpick οδοντογλυφίδα
Ⓞ-TH̲ⓄN-DⓄ-G̲LⒺⒺ-FⒺⒺ-THⓐⓗ

tour ξενάγηση KSⒺN-ⓐⓗ-YⒺⒺ-SⒺⒺ

tourist   τουρίστας   T⬤⬤-B︎ⓔⓔS-T⬤S

towel   πετσέτα   Pⓔ︎T-Sⓔ︎-T⬤

train   τρένο   TRⓔ︎-N⬤

travel agency   τουριστικό γραφείο

   T⬤⬤-B︎ⓔⓔS-T︎ⓔⓔ-K⬤   GB⬤-F︎ⓔⓔ-⬤

traveler's check   ταξιδιωτική επιταγή

   T⬤K-S︎ⓔⓔ-TH︎ⓔⓔ-⬤-T︎ⓔⓔ-K︎ⓔⓔ   ⓔ︎-P︎ⓔⓔ-T⬤-Y︎ⓔⓔ

trip   ταξίδι   T⬤K-S︎ⓔⓔ-TH︎ⓔⓔ

Tuesday   Τρίτη   TRⓔ︎-T︎ⓔⓔ

Turkey (country)   Τουρκία   T⬤⬤B-K︎ⓔⓔ-⬤

U

umbrella   ομπρέλα   ⬤M-BBⓔ︎-L⬤

understand (to)   καταλαβαίνω   K⬤-T⬤-L⬤-Vⓔ︎-N⬤

underwear   εσώρουχα   ⓔ︎-S⬤-B⬤⬤-H⬤

United Kingdom   Ἡνωμένο Βασίλειο

   ︎ⓔⓔ-N⬤-Mⓔ︎-N⬤   V⬤-S︎ⓔⓔ-L︎ⓔⓔ-⬤

United States   Ηνωμένες Πολιτείες

   ︎ⓔⓔ-N⬤-Mⓔ︎-N⬤   P⬤-L︎ⓔⓔ-Tⓔ︎-ⓔⓔS

university   πανεπιστήμιο   P⬤-Nⓔ︎-P︎ⓔⓔS-T︎ⓔⓔ-M︎ⓔⓔ-⬤

up   επάνω - ψηλά   ⓔ︎-P⬤-N⬤ - PS︎ⓔⓔ-L⬤

urgent   επείγον   ⓔ︎-P︎ⓔⓔ-G⬤N

V

vacant ελεύθερο ⓔ-Lⓔ́F-THⓔ-Rⓞ

vacation διακοπές TH㉐-ⓐ-Kⓞ-Pⓔ́S

valuable πολύτιμος Pⓞ-Lⓔ́-T㉐-MⓞS

value αξία ⓐK-S㉐-ⓐ

vanilla βανίλια Vⓐ-N㉐-L-Yⓐ

veal μοσχάρι MⓞS-Hⓐ-R㉐

vegetables λαχανικά Lⓐ-Hⓐ-N㉐-Kⓐ

view θέα THⓔ́-ⓐ

vinegar ξύδι KS㉐́-TH㉐

W

wait! περίμενε Pⓔ-R㉐́-Mⓔ-Nⓔ

waiter σερβιτόρος SⓔR-V㉐-Tⓞ́-RⓞS

waitress σερβιτόρα SⓔR-V㉐-Tⓞ́-Rⓐ

want (I) θέλω THⓔ́-Lⓞ

wash (I) πλένω PLⓔ́-Nⓞ-Mⓔ

water νερό Nⓔ́-Rⓞ́

watermelon καρπούζι KⓐR-Pⓞⓞ-Z㉐

we εμείς ⓔ-M㉐S

weather καιρός Kⓔ-Rⓞ́S

Wednesday Τετάρτη Tⓔ-Tⓐ́R-T㉐

week εβδομάδα ⓔV-THⓞ-Mⓐ-THⓐ

welcome υποδοχή Pⓞ-THⓞ-H㉐

well done (cooked) καλοψημένη
Kah-LO-PSEE-MEE-NO

west Δύση THEE-SEE

wheelchair αναπηρική καρέκλα
ah-Nah-PEE-REE-KEE Kah-REE-KLah

when? πότε PO-TEE

where? που POO

which? ποιο PEE-O

white άσπρο ahS-PRO

who? ποιος PEE-OS

why? γιατί Yah-TEE

wife σύζυγος SEE-ZEE-GOS

wind άνεμος ah-NEE-MahS

window παράθυρο Pah-Rah-THEE-RO

wine κρασί KRah-SEE

Winter Χειμώνας HEE-MO-NahS

with με MEE

woman γυναίκα YEE-NEE-Kah

wonderful θαυμάσια THahV-Mah-SEE-ah

world κόσμος KOS-MOS

wrong λάθος Lah-TOS

XYZ

year έτος / χρόνος ℇ-TOS / HRO-NOS

yellow κίτρινο KℇE-TRℇE-NO

yes ναι Nℇ

yesterday εχθές ℇH-THℇS

you εσύ ℇ-Sℇ

zipper φερμουάρ FℇR-MOO-ahR

zoo ζωολογικός κήπος
  ZO-O-LO-Yℇ-KOS KℇE-POS

THANKS!

The nicest thing you can say to anyone in any language is "Thank you." Try some of these languages using the incredible Vowel Symbol System.

Spanish	French
GR@h-S@-@hS	M@R-S@

German	Italian
D@N-K@h	GR@hT-S@-@

Japanese	Chinese
D@-M@	SH@@ SH@@

Swedish	Portuguese
TⓐⓗK	Ⓞ-BRⒺⒺ-Gⓐⓗ-DⓄ

Arabic	Greek
SHⓄⓄ-KRⓐⓗN	ⓔF-Hⓐⓗ-RⒺⒺ-STⓄ

Hebrew	Russian
TⓄ-Dⓐⓗ	SPⓐⓗ-SⒺⒺ-Bⓐⓗ

Swahili	Dutch
ⓐⓗ-SⓐⓗN-TⒶ	DⓐⓗNK ⓄⓄ

Tagalog	Hawaiian
Sⓐⓗ-Lⓐⓗ-MⓐⓗT	Mⓐⓗ-Hⓐⓗ-LⓄ

INDEX